Ixion

Morton Feldman, Notation, Performance Practice and Jackson Pollock

Ixion

Morton Feldman, Notation, Performance Practice and Jackson Pollock

John Snijders

Marmalade Publishers of Visual Theory

John Snijders is a pianist and associate professor of music performance at Durham University. He studied piano, fortepiano and composition at Royal Conservatoire Den Haag, founded the Ives Ensemble in 1986 and was a member of the Nieuw Ensemble Amsterdam between 1988 and 2013.

Figures

The degree to which a music's notation is responsible for much of the composition itself, is one of history's best kept secrets.

Morton Feldman
Give My Regards to Eighth Street[1]

Introduction

Middelburg, Netherlands, July 1985.
Whilst studying at the Den Haag Royal Conservatoire, I decided to take a trip to the Festival Nieuwe Muziek Zeeland, which unbeknownst to me at the time, turned out to be the most defining experience of my musical development.

The Festival Nieuwe Muziek Zeeland was founded by the brilliant and indefatigable Ad van 't Veer in 1976 and is in a remote part of the Netherlands and was during this period a kind of secret event, catering for those interested in the more alternative side of the avant-garde. Regular guests have included over the years, Misha Mengelberg, Iannis Xenakis, John Cage and Morton Feldman.

During my time at the festival, I also met Morton Feldman for the first time, attended some of his extended talks,[2] and also heard the rehearsal of *Trio*, all done whilst Feldman systematically emptied the venue's bar fridge and instructed the musicians that it was "too loud!" and to make it sound "more sexy".

Even though I had by this time played a few of Feldman's earlier shorter pieces, my first experience of *Trio, For Christian*

Wolff, and *Piano, violin, viola, cello*, caused me to have a life-long fascination with Feldman's music, which started with the later pieces and then working my way back, reaching the earlier graph pieces, after quite a few years of developing ideas about the interpretation of his music.

Feldman's graph pieces were difficult to get my head round at first. Not because of the style of the notation, as all notation needs to be learnt, but because of the implications Feldman's compositions imply, regarding harmony, rhythm, and the radical freedom given to the performer to choose their own pitches without being given any idea to what the composer's preference might be, or if this would actually even matter.

I had worked with John Cage a number of times from 1988, until his death in 1992 and naturally thought that Cage's views on giving the performer their own responsibility and freedom would be valid for Feldman's work too. However, things turned out to be a lot more complicated than that.

Yes, they were close friends, at least until the early 1980s, but both Feldman and Cage's musical paths diverged, to the extent that Cage was increasingly negative about the direction of Feldman's music. For example, in 1972, after Cage performed as one of the five pianists in Feldman's *Pianos and Voices*, Cage told him angrily "You're an extremist! A poetic extremist!"[3] Feldman, however, continued to defend Cage, but it became clear that there were at least as many subjects in which their views conflicted, as they had ideas in common.

I met Feldman again at the Festival Nieuwe Muziek Zeeland in July 1987, and this time I was able to sit down with him for an hour or so and go over a number of his most recent scores in detail. Feldman was very patient with me and seemed to enjoy discussing his scores with a young pianist who was not daunted by the extended duration of these works. I had not looked at the graph scores by that point and so lamentably did not discuss these with him. A missed opportunity certainly, but then again, you only know these things way after the fact. I was also fortunate enough though, to also be present at the world premiere of Feldman's last finished piece, *Piano, violin, viola, cello*, and when afterwards I told Feldman how shatteringly beautiful it was, he said, "Thank you, a bit too much atmosphere, especially at the end."

Morton Feldman died aged 61, nine weeks after this meeting.

This work is the result of my meditations on the various problems Feldman's graph pieces throw up for performers, ranging from how to get to grips with the notational language and its musical implications, and the aesthetic and stylistic choices that need to be considered and why these are not immediately apparent from the scores themselves.

I have decided to focus within this text, on one of the lesser known pieces, Feldman's only work specifically written for the Merce Cunningham Dance Company, *Ixion*, as it not only is a perfect and clear example of a graph score, but due to the fact that it exists in two versions, one for chamber orchestra or large ensemble, and one for two pianos, with each needing their own distinct approach, it allows for both a focused discussion and a broader investigation on performance issues in pieces for small and larger forces. Each version leaves many decisions open to the performer, without being overly clear as to whether the performer should follow their own aesthetic preferences or if there are more complicated issues to consider.

To understand each version of *Ixion* in more detail, I have made a comparative analysis of each work to establish if they need to be seen as two versions of the same piece or if one might be a more thorough reworking of the other.

Also, as Feldman considered *Ixion* to be a work in which he came as close as he could to a piece that was composed in a similar way to how Jackson Pollock painted, I have also attempted to link Feldman's ideas about painting with composing, by looking at the work of Piet Mondrian, Philip Guston, Mark Rothko and Pollock.

The direct transfer of one art form and practice to another is of course very problematic indeed, and this has forced me to think about the idea of 'all-over' composition, flatness, colour, texture and many other factors that are used in both disciplines, but yet, could entail very different things.

Some elements in this book are an elaboration of the essay *That is not freedom, that is taking licence: The pitfalls in performing Morton Feldman's graph scores*, which I completed in 2019, arising from the conference *The Aesthetics of Imperfection in Music and the Arts* held on 6-7 October 2018, at The Black Swan, part of the Newcastle Arts Centre, organised by Andy Hamilton, Professor of Philosophy at Durham University. [4]

In Chapter 1, I discuss where Feldman's way of working may have come from, how he felt he learnt more from painters than from other composers (John Cage and Beethoven as notable exceptions), and how he came to the decision of developing a new notational system and how this system would differ from graphic notation.

Chapter 2 considers the two scores of *Ixion*, the history of the piece, the structure and comparison of the two existing versions, and relates this to the comparative analysis in the next chapter.

Within Chapter 4 I discuss the specifics of performing the piece, the various problems around the two scores and the issues for which performers will need to find their own solutions, which I argue, needs to be informed by the composer's aesthetics and preferences.

The Chapter 5 explores the possible links with Jackson Pollock's artistic practice and how this may have found its way into Feldman's *Ixion*.

Feldman
and Composing

Over and over again, in his talks, writings and interviews, Feldman comes back to how he feels that his way of thinking about composition has more to do with the way painters think about painting than how composers think about composing. He is convinced that there are ideas about the creative process composers do not know about, or are not aware of, and that for him are vital to the creative act.

It is not just thinking about the way a work is actually constructed, but a lot of the topics Feldman mentions are to do with the attitude towards making art. In several sources he laments the fact that composers are more interested with how a piece is made, than the actual sound of the work.

> Music is not painting, but it can learn from this more perceptive temperament that waits and observes the inherent mystery of its material, as opposed to the composer's vested interest in his craft. [...] The painter achieves mastery by allowing what he is doing to be itself. In a way, he must step aside in order to be in control. The composer is just learning to do this. He is just beginning to

learn that controls can be thought of as nothing more than accepted practice. [1]

It is Boulez, more than any composer today, who has given system a new prestige – Boulez, who once said in an essay that he is not interested in how a piece sounds, only in how it is made. No painter would talk that way. Philip Guston once told me that when he sees how a painting is made he becomes bored with it. [2]

Painters, you see, are not concerned with how a thing is made. They make. And then their stamina, their gift of survival. Musicians want to be fed from above. [3]

Ever since getting to know the Abstract Expressionist painters in early 1951, Feldman would hang out with them almost daily, mostly in the Cedar Street Tavern on University Place near Manhattan's Washington Square Park, where they would have long and intense discussion and arguments about painting. These would be of a deep and lasting influence on his way of thinking about music, composing and art, and he would refer to this period throughout his life. It is interesting to note that art critic Harold Rosenberg, who was not a very regular guest at the bar, at least a lot less regular than his fellow art critic and theorist Clement Greenberg, did not have a very high opinion of the level of discussion:

Philosophy is not popular among American painters. For most, thinking consists of the various arguments that TO PAINT is something different from, say, to write or to criticize: a mystique of the particular activity. Lacking verbal flexibility, the painters speak of what they are doing

> in a jargon still involved in the metaphysics of things: "My painting is not Art, it's an Is." It's not a picture of a thing; it's the thing itself." "It doesn't reproduce Nature; it is Nature." "The painter doesn't think, he knows." Etc, etc. "Art is not, not not not not..." As against this, a few reply, art today is the same as it always has been. [4]

Feldman's embrace of the painterly way of thinking about creating work does not, however, mean that he is not interested in systems per se, and it is also clear that he would not adhere to a romantic notion of 'divine inspiration' rather than of meticulous hard work, but it does show a strong commitment to the intuitive workings of dealing with material, and letting the material inform the composer's thought processes.

In an interview for VPRO Dutch Radio in 1985, Feldman said:

> "But I do have a system, and my system essentially is thought. It is a system, that is, it's a system in terms of, not as philosophy, but just thinking as I'm writing. Living thinking rather than dead thinking, or pre-thinking. I don't want to have the piece already written so I don't have anything to think about as I write it." [5]

This is close to the way Philip Guston worked in his abstract paintings, usually starting with just putting an almost random mark on the canvas, which became the starting point for a painterly composition that was not predetermined in any way, or Jackson Pollock's intuitive pouring of paint and enamel on the canvas whereby the work was formed during the actual making. This, however, should not be confused with a work being 'improvised'. Feldman did not have many good words to say about improvisation, even though his ideas of what improvisation is could be said to be somewhat limited. Feldman saw improvisation as something that would always be reliant on pre-existing forms, where there was no possibility of the kind of musical development he was looking for in his own music, which relied on a constant deep involvement with the act of conscious and concentrated flexibility of thinking.

> I don't feel that improvisation has that kind of flexibility that they feel that they have. That's all. I always wonder about the flexibility. It's either "in the style of..." [...] It's important to hear you saying that it does not have to do with spontaneity, but it might. So, it's the monolithical aspect. In other words: for me it's a little too monolithic. [...]
>
> *And chance...*
>
> No chance, working with the same structures all the time. In other words, there were no surprises in those structures just like there were no surprises in a Stockhausen structure. Because I saw from where it came, and I saw how it was made. [6]

The specific strategies Feldman employed when composing are all designed to facilitate the process of composing through thinking. In a lecture given at the Darmstädter Ferienkurse für Neue Musik in 1984, he lists a number of them: writing not in pencil but in ink, because it is a way of knowing the amount of concentration he has. Not keeping sketches. Copy out the bit of a composition right after having written it, as the process of copying out will give you the opportunity to develop other ideas. This strategy was given to him by John

Cage but could also have been inspired by his friend, the Austrian/American architect Frederick Kiesler. Feldman relates the story of Kiesler visiting an architecture department at a Texas university:

> He said, 'I went into this tremendous room, and on every desk, there was an electric sharpener. So all the kids there were sharpening their pencils.' Kiesler went, and he sat down at a desk, and he took out his old Viennese penknife, and he started to sharpen a pencil. And he said to them, 'All you did was sharpen a pencil.' He said, 'I just had an idea for a building.' [7]

> Having the right material, from the right kind of pen to the right kind of chair. Also he says "When I sit down and write a piece, I'm in thought. And as I'm moving, I'm focusing from one thought to another. And the whole idea of being in thought is to find the right kinds of notation at that moment that presents that thought. [8]

Of course, these practicalities do not give any information on the specific nature of Feldman's composing, in that it does not say anything about choice, about the outside influences that would inform or not inform his composing, or on style. Here, Feldman proves to be a very elusive composer and analysing his work in these respects is practically doomed to failure. It is always possible to analyse the works on a bureaucratic level, that is, to make an inventory of everything that happens in a piece and making tables and lists of these, but attempts to finding any kind of rule-based system is almost guaranteed to fail. Or, as Christian Wolff puts it:

> Feldman, arguably, has no ideas. In a way, he's just Feldman. He's very hard to appropriate. [9]

It is interesting to see that one of the attempts at analysis, a graphic representation of Feldman's *String Quartet (II)* from 1983, produced by Walter Zimmermann and printed in *Morton Feldman, Essays* (fig. 1), which in appearance at least, has quite strong links with the graph pieces in their grid structure. Feldman himself liked the drawing a lot. He said about it:

> It's not a painting. This is an analysis of the quartet where the information duplicates itself and comes back in variation. [...] It's just a duplication graphically on the kind of material that comes and goes in the piece. It's an aspect of something called the 'new criticism', like counting commas. And I learned a lot. I like to see it. [10]

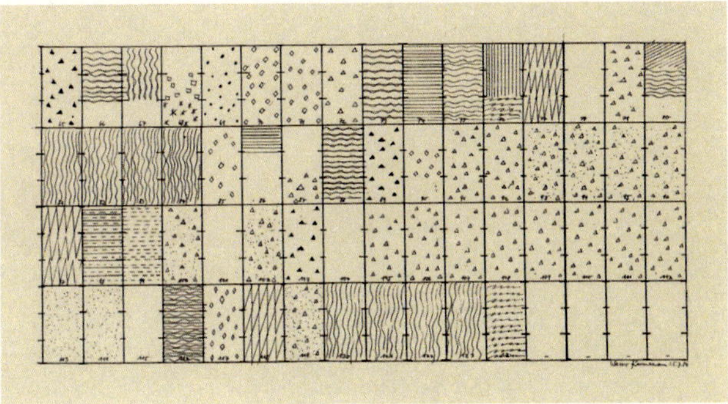

FIGURE 1

Walter Zimmermann, *Analysis of a string quartet*, page 2 (1985).

Throughout his compositional career Feldman's way of composing through thinking has been a constant feature. The pieces would naturally change in various aspects. Their length evolved from mostly short or very short pieces in the 1950s and 1960s, getting into a 25-minute average in the 1970s to the expanded length of an hour or more from 1979 onwards. The harmonic language could fluctuate between very sparse to very dense, but always very chromatic with no sense of a tonal centre. In some pieces there are hints of some tonal (although they are actually usually more modal) melodic elements, like in *The Viola in my Life 2* (1970) and *Rothko Chapel* (1971) and in his late works the harmony in general is a lot more transparent.

In the graph pieces we can only measure density, since in these pieces harmony is necessarily a result of the choices the performer makes at the time of performing, so they could be said to be exceptions to this. Nevertheless, there is a case to be made to maintain the same kind of harmonic language even here.

Other features which have remained constant throughout his compositional output: Feldman's instrumentation has always been focused on using traditional instruments in traditional ways. There are no pieces using extended techniques (if one considers glissandi to be part of string and wind players' standard techniques, and even then, he uses them only sparingly, generally not exceeding a semitone), and Feldman does not use instruments that he feels are not fitting to his idea of instrumental colour.

There are no pieces in which Feldman uses saxophones, and the inclusion of percussion other than standard orchestral percussion instruments is extremely rare. There is an amplified guitar in the orchestral piece *Marginal Intersection* (1951), a piece that through its use of oscillators, recorded sounds and non-standard percussion instruments is very much an exception in his œuvre, owing a lot to specific influences by Cage and possibly Varèse. The guitar also features in the 1961 ensemble work *The Straits of Magellan*. No brass instruments are used other than the standard orchestral ones, and again only very rarely does Feldman use an electric guitar (in 1966 he worked with Christian Wolff on a piece for this instrument called *The Possibility of a New Work for Electric Guitar*, the score of which was lost and only reconstructed by Seth Josel in 2013, using the recording made of Wolff's performance in 1967).

Feldman only made one single foray into electronic music, *Intersection for Magnetic Tape* (1953), a piece with which he was very dissatisfied. The dynamic range of his music from 1950 onwards tends to be quiet or extremely quiet, although there are some pieces with extremely loud moments, that seem mostly to function as either irritants (Feldman admitted to me during a meeting in Middelburg in 1987 that the single triple-forte chord in *Trio* (1981) was there mainly 'to irritate people') or as a kind of musical punctuation, as in *Piano* (1977).

There are a handful of works that have a more varied dynamic range, such as *String Quartet* (1979) and *String Quartet (II)* (1983), and the general dynamic of *Words and Music* (1987) is mezzo piano with the louder fragments being mezzo forte. Also, some of the graph pieces have a different dynamic range, notably *Intersection 2 & 3* (1951 and 1953) where the player is free to choose any dynamics, and *Ixion* where the performers are free to play occasional loud sounds, but otherwise, as Feldman said:

> What is Morton Feldman, he is quiet. And now he is quiet and long. Before he used to be quiet and short, now he is quiet and long. [11]

The reasons for writing mostly quiet music do not feature very often in his writings and talks. A possibility could be that the low dynamic level is related to the surface structure of most Abstract Expressionist painting. There was a preference for a flatness in the picture plane, and a notable absence of impasto, making the work as two-dimensional as possible. According to Clement Greenberg, one of the most important theorists of the Abstract Expressionists:

> It was the stressing of the ineluctable flatness of the surface that remained, however, more fundamental than anything else to the processes by which pictorial art criticized and defined itself under Modernism. For flatness alone was unique and exclusive to pictorial art. The enclosing shape of the picture was a limiting condition, or norm, that was shared with the art of the theatre; colour was a norm and a means shared not only with the theatre, but also with sculpture. Because flatness was the only condition painting shared with no other art, Modernist painting oriented itself to flatness as it did to nothing else.[12]

Even though Greenberg does not associate flatness with music, the influence the Abstract Expressionists and Piet Mondrian had on Feldman's thinking made him search for a way of flattening out his musical surfaces in order to get the musical material as abstract as it could possibly be. It is not true that his music was quiet from the start, but we do see that from the moment the painters' thoughts became more important sources of ideas for him, the dynamic level of his music settled down. Also, in quite a few of the scores from the 1950's and 60's we see the instruction 'a minimum of attack'. This might be an equivalent of the way the edges of the colour fields in a lot of the Abstract Expressionist painters' work (Mark Rothko, Barnett Newman, Robert Motherwell, Philip Guston) was seldom sharply defined, but more often than not would bleed and feather out. A sound made with as little edge as possible would be a possible aural counterpart. Especially Rothko and Guston tended to use fairly muted colours (not always, but quite often), and Rothko would prefer his work to be hung in a space with low-level lighting, which made the quietness of the work even stronger. This too could be something Feldman was hoping to achieve in his music by keeping the dynamics low and the attack minimal. Cage and Feldman discuss the dynamic range of Feldman's music in the WBAI Radio conversation of 16 January 1967, where Cage asks:

> You remember, years ago, there were sporadic loud sounds. What made them disappear?
>
> MF: I think they existed as some form of punctuation.
>
> JC: That you felt was no longer necessary?
>
> MF: Yes.
>
> JC: Really?
>
> MF: I think that I was still involved – I don't remember – but I think I was still involved with some elements of differentiation.
>
> JC: They'd be, wouldn't they, like the opposite of punctuation, since, by being louder, they would stand out?
>
> MF: Exclamation points (laugh). I don't know what happened, John. Maybe I heard too much of its attack,

maybe I didn't hear, maybe I have some notion about the purity of the sound itself being lost in the loudness of the attack.

JC: At any rate, it appeared to you as unnecessary to the rest of the music?

MF: Yes. It also, in a sense, created a certain amount of energy that I felt I had to use. They became an interference of some kind. [13]

Feldman did quite often remark on purely compositional choice-making. On multiple occasions he would make it clear that it is impossible for him to write down a note if he doesn't know the specific octave and the specific instrument that will play it. He says he is not involved with style at all, relating it to painting, and that his music, with that of Cage, is actually the purest music being written:

> And Philip's[14] main theme, or if it's not his main theme it's his main concern, let's put it this way, was the impossibility of painting a picture today, that it is actually impossible to paint something today because to some degree everything has already been painted. A lot of people feel there is no problem, they just find their style and they just paint that style, but if you don't begin with style, and you say 'I want to paint a picture', and your cop-out is not a look or a style, then it's pretty impossible to think about what in heaven's name am I gonna paint? And I think what my music demonstrates for me, I have no idea really you know, what other people really hear in it, but what my music really demonstrates for me is the impossibility of going ahead and just writing a purely abstract piece of music that is not for example metamusic, or involved with so many things

> that are extraneous to music. One of the most interesting things about this point of view is that I once got into an argument, when I first started to go to Europe, and people would say "but this is not music". And I would say "Well", I said, "I think that John Cage and myself are the only ones that are really writing music, because we are not doing anything else." [15]

More directly and concretely, we get some idea of his way of working when Feldman states:

> In fact I have found ways to arrive at concentration. One of the most important ways is that I write in ink. So, if I begin to work and I see that I am crossing out ime [sic! – possibly 'time'], I realize in a sense that I thought I was concentrated, but in fact I wasn't concentrated. So, the writing in ink is an inner parameter to how concentrated I really am. And then I go ahead and write the piece, again using the ink as a parameter. And if I see that I'm crossing out, I just leave the piece and go to it at another time. So, to me that concentration is more important than someone else's pitch organization or whatever conceptual attitude they have about the piece. [...] I think there are three things working with me: my ears, my mind and my fingers. I don't think that it's just ear. That would mean that I'm just improvising, and I'm writing down what I like, or I'm writing down what I don't like. But those three parameters are always at work.[16]

Still, the problem of not wanting to think about style is one that ultimately Feldman did not think he was able to solve, especially when looking at his own work in hindsight. In a public conversation with Philip Guston in 1968 he admits:

> I don't want to have a point of view. But it's impossible. I was listening to some old music. My old Columbia record[17] is being reissued; it's coming out in January. So I was up there today, and I didn't hear a lot of those things for a long time. And I said to myself, I thought I was working within a nonstyle. I was interested in just the material, just let them speak, and I had no style. I actually felt when I was writing it that I was anonymous. And now I listen to the stuff and it's the way I felt after looking at Kandinsky when I was mature, and first seeing him when I was about eleven. I saw it when I was eleven; it was free. I saw it when I was an adult and it was commercial art. [laughter] So I listened to my stuff and it was just classy style! Elegant, everything. The way it was phrased, everything fit in place.[18]

The Graph Pieces

Between 1950 and 1967, Feldman wrote 17 pieces, or 18 if we consider the two versions of *Ixion* as separate works, for which he designed a totally new notational system.[19]

Both he and John Cage describe in separate sources, how the invention was almost a casual act, done while waiting at Cage's apartment for dinner to be ready. Feldman's recollection:

> But the initial concept of the grid – Oh, it's like one of those things that you don't know is going to have significance afterwards. I have no idea how it came about. Actually, I was living in the same building as John Cage

> and he invited me to dinner. And it wasn't ready yet. John was making wild rice the way most people don't know how it should be made. That is, just waiting for boiling water and then putting new boiling water into the rice and then having another pot boiling and then draining the rice, etc., etc., so we were waiting a long time for the wild rice to be ready. It was while waiting for the wild rice that I just sat down at his desk and picked up a piece of note paper and started to doodle. And what I doodled was a freely drawn page of graph paper – and what emerged were high, middle and low categories. It was just automatic – I never had any conversation about it heretofore, you know – never discussed it. [20]

Cage remembers it more or less similar:

> when I was living in new york I was often with david tudor morton feldman christian wolff earle brown in the place where I lived that had a beautiful view of the east river and virtually no furniture one room with a piano in it and the other room was where I slept morton feldman went into the room with the piano and I stayed at my desk which was in the bedroom with david tudor shortly morton feldman came back with his first piece of graph music where on graph paper he simply put numbers and indicated high middle and low how many high notes how many middle notes how many low notes and nothing else there were squares that he left empty so there were no notes there at all after he showed it to me and to david tudor david tudor went to the piano and played it it was a great experience"[21]

Even though the actual invention was a matter of minutes, the process leading up to this was at least a few years in the making and was the result of not only thinking very carefully about the nature of notation and the need to free sounds from the composer, but also of Feldman's deep and strong involvement with the tight group of New York-based painters, usually referred to as the "Abstract Expressionists", and their work. The following paragraphs discuss the various strands of musical, and non-musical thinking leading to the highly individual way of notating music that can be seen as the first example of a purely graphic notation for compositional and performance purposes. As Christian Wolff said in 1969:

> The first one of us, however, who really went in for indeterminacy in performance was Feldman with those pieces written on graph paper where the range of the instrument is divided into high, middle and low, and the performer can pick any note from the specified register. Feldman has dropped indeterminacy nowadays, and he must always have looked at it very differently from Cage. [22]

Cage acknowledged the fact that Feldman's graph pieces opened up a whole new way of thinking, in one of the conversations they had for WBAI Radio New York in 1966:

> JC: I think I expressed once the idea that you had discovered a world, a musical world – because it was your music, really, that opened up everything, your piece, what was it called, I think the first one was for piano…
>
> MF: "Projection."
>
> JC: "Projection", yes. And you write it down at Monroe Street and David Tudor and I were in the other room. You

> left us and you wrote this piece on graph, giving us the freedom of playing in these three ranges – high, middle, and low – and then we went in and played the piece, and it was then that the musical world changed. Now not just the musical world inside you, in this role that you speak of, deep in thought. Nevertheless, the thing I think I said to you once on that walk through the night is, now that you have opened up this world, let us see all the things that are in it. [23]

Even though *Projection 1* is for solo cello, it is entirely possible that the sketch Feldman made at the gathering at Cage's apartment was for piano, given that David Tudor was present. Feldman's insistence that he could not write anything down without knowing which instrument was playing might indicate that this first attempt at making a graphic score was not thought of as a non-specified attempt, but as a piece for piano. However, it is not sure if this sketch has survived. There is an untitled sketch of two systems of hand-drawn graph music in the John Cage Collection at Northwestern University Music Library (Evanston, Ill., USA), but it is not known if this is indeed the sketch made at Cage's apartment.

Feldman's need for a totally new way of music notation is best described in his article *Predeterminate/Indeterminate*, in which he says:

> Between 1950 and 1951 four composers – John Cage, Earle Brown, Christian Wolff and myself – became friends, saw each other constantly – and something happened. Joined by the pianist David Tudor, each of us in his own way contributed to a concept of music in which various

> elements (rhythm, pitch, dynamics, etc.) were decontrolled. Because this music was not "fixed," it could not be notated in the old way. Each new thought, each new idea within this thought, suggested its own notation. [24]

This concept of music being decontrolled could be said to have started with John Cage's interest in aspects of Eastern philosophy, brought about by his meetings with Gita Sarabhai, an Indian musician who, being concerned with what she felt was the ever-increasing influence of Western music on the music traditions of India, went in 1946 to study in the USA to try and understand 'the enemy' better. She and Cage met on an almost daily basis, Cage teaching her about Western counterpoint and contemporary music, and Sarabhai teaching him about traditional Indian music and its philosophies.

Sarabhai's reply to his question on the function of writing music was one of the catalysts for his development of the concept of freedom and letting go of control:

> To sober the mind and thus make it susceptible to divine influences.[25]

This led Cage to believe that a sober mind is equally at ease in noisy environments than in quiet ones, and that divine influences are all the things that happen in creation. From here, he started to read more about Indian philosophy, leading to his acceptance of:

> [...] the doctrine about Art, occidental and oriental, set forth by Ananda K. Coomaraswamy in his book The Transformation of Nature in Art, that the function of Art is to imitate Nature in her manner of operation. [26]

Although Cage says that in the late 1940s he started to attend classes by the renowned Zen scholar Daisetz Teitaro Suzuki, it seems that Suzuki did not actually start teaching in New York until 1950.[27] Even so, his involvement with Zen thinking led Cage to be more and more convinced of the need that:

> [...] my work would change me, would free me from my likes and dislikes.[28]

This resulted in a way of composing with chance operations, using the *I Ching* as a means of obtaining the decisions he felt he should no longer make himself, which, depending on the initial idea for the piece, could lead to hyper-determined pieces such as *Music of Changes* (1951) and hyper-undetermined pieces such as *Concert for Piano and Orchestra* (1957/1958). However, the first piece Cage wrote which is no longer in standard music notation and has elements of non-determinate graphic scoring is *Williams Mix* (1952), a piece for tape, which would by its very nature need a different way of notation anyway. This is two years after Feldman wrote his first graph score. It is clear from reading Cage's *Lecture on Something*, that Feldman's decision to forego control over pitch was of immense influence on Cage, and subsequently changed the way he himself composed:

> Feldman speaks of no sounds and takes within broad limits the first ones that come along. He has changed the responsibility of the composer from making to accepting. To accept whatever comes regardless of the consequences is to be unafraid or to be full of that love which comes from a sense of at-one-ness with whatever. This goes to explain what Feldman means when he says that he is associated

> with all of the sounds, and so can foresee what will happen even though he has not written the particular notes down as other composers do. [29]

For Feldman the decision to let go of controlling some aspects of decision-making in his compositions has nothing to do with oriental thinking.

> My whole debt to Oriental culture is Chinese food. [30]

Feldman's remark is perhaps somewhat exaggerated and perhaps even flippant but does indicate his influences lie elsewhere. John Cage's influence on Feldman's thinking was substantial, so it can be assumed at least some of Cage's ideas informed his view on composing, but he always maintained that his musical thinking comes from a staunchly European tradition:

> But I think John's Zenness is not so intense. I think, again, just like the way Surrealism in a sense opened up the mind, John said one should keep one's mind open for divine influences. I think John's Zen really comes from the fact that he grew up on the West Coast, which faces the Orient. New York faces Germany; that's why the tradition in New York was essentially Germanic. [31]

Feldman elaborates on his reasons to do away with controlling pitch, and to a certain extent rhythm, in a few articles and talks. Some of these deal with Cage's influence and, as he called it, the way Cage gave him "permissions to have confidence in my instincts"[32], some with the change in thinking brought about by his intense involvement with the

Abstract Expressionist painters, and some purely with musical thought. One clear description of what he felt needed to be done can again be found in *Predeterminate/Indeterminate*:

> Up to now the various elements of music (rhythm, pitch, dynamics, etc.) were only recognizable in terms of their formal relationship to each other. As controls are given up, one finds that these elements lose their initial, inherent identity. But it is just because of this identity that these elements can be unified within the composition. Without this identity there can be no unification. It follows then, that an indeterminate music can lead only to catastrophe. This catastrophe we allowed to take place. Behind it was sound – which unified everything. Only by "unfixing" the elements traditionally used to construct a piece of music could the sounds exist in themselves – not as symbols, or memories which were memories of other music to begin with. [33]

Feldman, together with Cage, Wolff and Brown, clearly searched for a way of dealing with what they felt was an obsession of contemporary composers with ordering every element in every work, something that was heavily impeding sound itself to be free. This might be seen as a direct response to the insistence of the main players on the European (read Darmstadt [34]) scene (Pierre Boulez, Karlheinz Stockhausen, Luigi Nono, Karel Goeyvaerts) on the absolute importance and necessity of total serialism, in which all parameters of a composition are subjected to the strictest possible rules. However, strict, or total serialism really only dates from 1951, and so was not around yet as they came up with their attempts to free up sound. It is entirely possible to see the antagonism towards this way of thinking as an attempt to distinguish the American contemporary composers from their European colleagues. The serialist way of thinking had made it to the US by way of people like Stefan Wolpe, a German composer who fled the Nazi regime and established himself as an important New York teacher (Feldman was actually one of his students).

There were composers like Milton Babbitt, whose *Three Compositions for Piano* (1947) already has a lot of strict serial elements, and to some degree Elliott Carter too, who also took some of the ideas of serialists' hyper-organization on board. However, in 1950 Carter was not yet seen as an important figure, and Babbitt was teaching mathematics, not music, so their influence was limited and not part of the mainstream compositional thinking. Wolpe's serialism was never as strict as what the Darmstadt composers were advocating. Wolpe, after his brief studies with Anton Webern, had arrived at a very idiosyncratic technique of using tone-rows, often not 12-tone rows but either shorter or longer rows, where emphasis was more on intervallic relationships than on not repeating pitches until all other 11 had sounded.

Wolpe did not use rows to order colour, dynamics, and rhythm, but he did use all kinds of other rule-based systems in his later works, from around 1949 onwards. His direct influence on Feldman's music can be clearly seen in the use of some specific harmonic characteristics, but otherwise is not directly clear, with a few exceptions, such as the piano piece *Illusions* (1949).

It is important to understand too that Feldman only really got to know the New York painters and their work in early 1951 when he visited the exhibition *Abstract Painting and Sculpture in America* at the Museum of Modern Art, New York in 1951 with Cage.

Cage subsequently introduced Feldman to Philip Guston and soon after Robert Rauschenberg, which would be why he talks about *Projection 2* rather than *1* in the following quote, as *Projection 1* was written before he got acquainted with the visual art that would be so instrumental to the development of his artistic ideas.

Even so, the matter is slightly confused, as the score of *Projection 2* stated 3 January 1951 as completion date, so this would date the piece before his introduction to Guston and Rauschenberg and their social circle. Actually *Projections 1* to *4* are all dated before 23 January 1951, and *Projection 5* just has the year, without a date, so it's not clear when this was finished. Feldman might have referred then more to Mondrian's influence than to the Abstract Expressionists, but it is hard to be sure – Feldman's chronology is not always very reliable. Besides, he is not explicitly talking about the Abstract Expressionists, but about 'new painting' in general, when he states:

> The new painting made me desirous of a sound world more direct, more immediate, more physical than anything that had existed heretofore. [...] The new structure required a concentration more demanding than if the technique were that of still photography, which for me is what precise notation has come to imply.
>
> *Projection II for flute, trumpet, violin and cello* [35] – one of the first graph pieces – was my first experience with this new thought. My desire was not to 'compose', but to project sounds into time, free from a compositional rhetoric that had no place here. In order not to involve the performer (i.e. myself) in memory (relationships), and because

> the sounds no longer had an inherent symbolic shape, I allowed for indeterminacies in regard to pitch. [36]

An interesting remark here is that when he talks about the performer he adds "i.e. myself", the implication being that the composer is not just the person writing down the piece, but he is the same time performing it. *Projection 2* (the printed text uses a Roman numeral, but the published manuscript shows an Arabic one) is a piece of chamber music for 5 performers, so the physical impossibility of Feldman being the only actual performer would necessitate a different view on what a performer actually is. As he was at the time of writing the text this quote is taken from (1964) still very much thinking about Jackson Pollock and his specific way of painting, it can be argued that he thought the act of composing, the act of physically putting the marks on the paper, is in itself a performance, in the way Pollock's way of painting had a strong performative side. Therefore, the musicians who would be involved with making the piece audible are not necessarily the performers Feldman talks about.

In the same article he makes it clear that leaving performers to choose the exact pitches is not the same as providing freedom for the composer:

> For myself, most of my observations about my work are after the fact, and a technical discussion of my methodology would be quite misleading. I do not feel I am being 'free' when I use a process that gives up control of pitches in one composition, rhythm and dynamics in another, etc., etc. Thus, I am left in a suspended state with regard to my role, but in a hopeful one with regard to the eventual outcome. What I control is my will – something far more difficult

> than a page of music. If I want my music to demonstrate anything, it is that 'nature and human nature are one'. [37]

According to Christian Wolff:

> [...] there was Feldman, and Feldman was doing those graph pieces and in some ways they're not at all indeterminate when you get back far enough because that's the way, he just worked with sonorities, he didn't care about the pitches and, you know, he wanted a high flute, you know, you just make that little square high and that's a high flute. You didn't have to worry if it was an E-flat or an F-sharp. That was secondary. But it was, on the other hand, the notion at the time was very shocking to people. They were like, "What? You're not telling the flute what note to play?" [laughs] And so I think Feldman in that sense was the first person specifically to do something like that. [38]

Leaving pitch undetermined for the composer is not quite the same thing as leaving the pitch undetermined for the performer, and Feldman is known to have been very unhappy with the way performers sometimes abused the freedom they were given.

> After several years of writing graph music, I began to discover its most important flaw. I was not only allowing the sounds to be free – I was also liberating the performer. I have never thought of the graph as an art of improvization, but more as a totally abstract sonic adventure. This realization was important because I now understood that if the performers sounds bad it was less because of

their lapses of taste than because I was still involved with passages and continuity that allowed their presence to be felt. [39]

Even though he blamed himself rather than the performer for this, he did find it difficult to deal with performers who mistook freedom for license. Further discussion on this can be found in Chapter 4.

Feldman had other issues with his graph music too:

MF: One of the problems about my chance music is that essentially it was too conceptual.

Walter Zimmermann: It's like one of the paintings hanging on the wall here, like Rauschenberg and those...)

MF: Yes, well, they were my friends. They were my friends. But not only that. There's something about a concept that is hard to break into. So, you have an image. And then you leave it alone. One of the big problems in my work was that, you know, as everything started to go into motion, I always felt that the performers in a sense were sensitive as to how to play the sounds, but they were not listening. And they were not sensitive to the pauses I give. So, the reason my music is notated is I wanted to keep control of the silence, you see. [40]

We see that after a few years of writing graph pieces Feldman stopped making them for a while, coinciding with a relatively unproductive period. His work list shows a total of 32 compositions written between 1950-1953 (4 unpublished to date), where the first 11 graph pieces were done, and just 14 in the years 1954-1957, (3 unpublished) in which no graph pieces were written. From 1958 until 1967 another 6 (or 7 if both

Ixion versions are counted as separate works) graph pieces saw the light of day, but in these years they were clearly only a small part of his total output of 51 compositions, of which 13 remain unpublished.[41] The majority of the non-graph works from the period 1950-1953 are conventionally notated, but we see a clear shift from 1958 onwards, where Feldman started using a way of notating that was, in a way, almost the opposite of the graph pieces. Instead of leaving the pitch undetermined, but the rhythm mostly fixed – although in some works, like the *Intersections for piano*, he merely states that the attacks should occur within the box but doesn't specify an exact placement –, he now fixes the pitch material but leaves the rhythm, the length of the notes, up to the performer. In some pieces he specifies:

> Durations of simultaneous and single sounds are extremely slow. All sounds connected without pauses unless notated.[42]

And in others he goes one step further:

> The first sound with both instruments simultaneously. The duration of each sound is chosen by the performer. [43]

In the latter notational method this necessarily will result in losing not only compositional control over timing, but also foregoing most of the control over the resulting harmony. Only from the 1969 orchestral piece *On Time and the Instrumental Factor* did Feldman return more or less completely to a conventional way of notating, in which all parameters are fixed. Exceptions are *Five Pianos* (1972) and *Pianos and Voices* (1972), which are closer to the notation used in *Durations*

2. There are some late pieces where he let go of the vertical alignment once more *Why Patterns?* (1978), *Crippled Symmetry* (1983), but here the music for each of the performers is still precisely notated, in rhythm and in pitch.

Notation

All the graph pieces are notated using a grid of squares, although the grid itself is not visible per se in some of the earliest works. The *Projection series* all have an implicit grid, but any boxes without information, that is containing rests, are not left blank, but completely removed from the score, so that the overall view is one of partial systems. (Fig. 2)

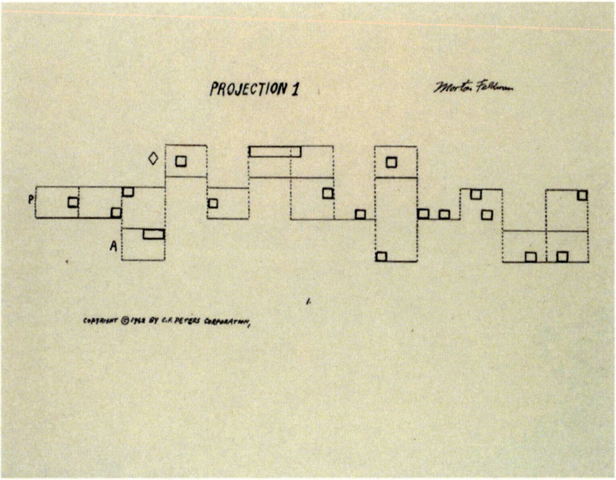

FIGURE 2

Morton Feldman, *Projection 1 for solo cello*, page 1 (1951).

Each box (in this piece there are three layers of boxes, the top one for harmonics, the middle for pizzicato, the bottom one for arco sounds) is vertically divided into three layers, indicating high, middle, and low register. Each box is four icti in length, with sub-boxes of one or more icti indicating the length of the sounds to be performed.

Apart from only the boxes with sounding material being visible, he also does not close the box if there is only a sound indicated either in the high or in the low register. This 'open box' notation is used in *Projection 1* and *Projection 4*, and for one system in *Projection 3*. In *Projection 2* there are some open boxes, but mostly they are closed, although the non-articulated ones are still left out. In the rest of *Projection 3* and *Projection 5*, all boxes are fully closed, possibly to provide a better legibility of the score. (Fig. 3)

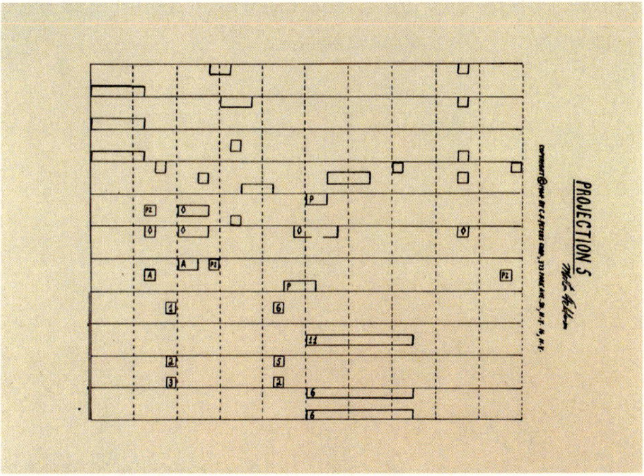

FIGURE 3

Morton Feldman, *Projection 5*, page 1 (1951).

The same notation was used for *Intersection 1* and *Marginal Intersection*, but from then on Feldman switches to a different visual structure. For *Intersection 2, 3* and *4*, the grid structure was fully notated, whether or not a box had sounds in it or not. Also, where the earlier scores had boxes that were divided in four icti, now every box is one single ictus, thereby removing any idea of a bar-like structure. Every ictus is equal to any other, and there is no implicit 4/4 bar present. Furthermore, Feldman started to put in numbers, indicating how many sounds are to be articulated. (Fig. 4)

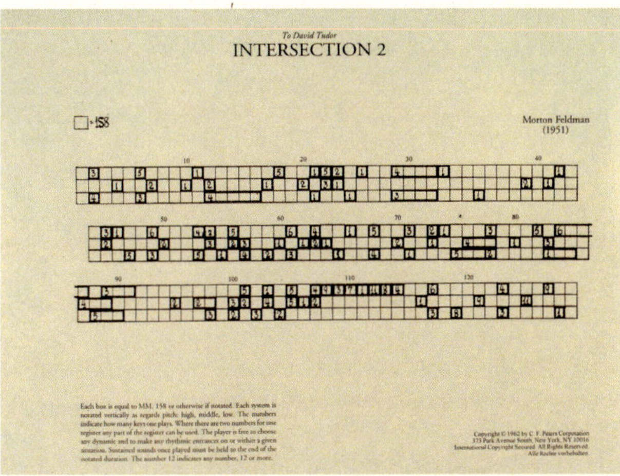

FIGURE 4

Morton Feldman, *Intersection 2 for piano*, page 1 (1951).

In addition to this negation of any metric structure, the rules governing rhythm changed as well. In the earlier graph pieces, all sounds are played at the start of the ictus and held (when possible) for the duration of the box. Now the performer is free to enter anywhere within the box, where sustained sounds (if chosen) are to be held until the end of the box. Note that the instruction does not say all notes are to be sustained, but clearly the performer has a choice to either play short notes, or notes of some duration, whereby the duration is prescribed by a combination of a freely chosen entry point and the length of the box. This non-metric box notation was also used for the later graph pieces, with some alterations when needed. In some pieces individual parts would have a partial grid, where longer durations are shown by longer boxes (rectangles instead of squares). This can be explained by another feature of the graph notation, which governs the register of the sounds to be played. In most graph pieces for chamber forces each instrument has three rows of boxes, indicating high, middle and low sounds. Here it is unproblematic to show every box, and only take out the dividing lines for longer durations. In other pieces, usually for larger forces, there is only one row of boxes per instrument, which means that necessarily the dividing lines will interrupt the strict square's structure. (Fig. 6)

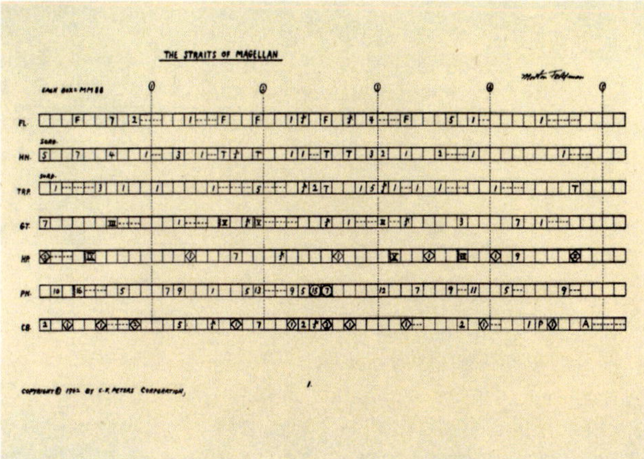

FIGURE 5

Morton Feldman, *The Straits of Magellan*, page 1 (1961).

The ensemble version of *Ixion* is another example of this type of notation, although in this piece durations no longer exist at all, which would be in line with Feldman's desire to write a piece that was more pointillistic in character.

In addition to providing numbers in the boxes denoting the specific number of sounds to be articulated, in later pieces Feldman started using all kinds of extra signs, but a discussion of these would fall outside the scope of this text. More information on these notational elements can be found in David Cline's book, *The Graph Music of Morton Feldman*. [44]

When Feldman showed the first graph pieces to John Cage, Cage felt that more attention should be given to the actual notation. He thought that Feldman's handwriting needed improvement and needed to be neater in style for the graph notation to work, and he offered to copy some of them out to show Feldman how to do this. Cage provided the fair copy for *Projection 4* and *Intersection 2*.

One important catalyst for making Feldman use a grid structure for his notation came from seeing the work of the Dutch painter Piet Mondrian:

> The whole secret is: if you understand Mondrian you'll understand me. I begin with nothing and arrive at everything, just like Mondrian, rather than starting with everything and arriving at nothing [laughs]. Just look at Mondrian, especially the early plus-minus [compositions] and the intervals and everything, how he feels his way. A kind of secret mathematics in terms of proportion, time. I think the big problem is that I learned more from painters that I learned from composers. [45]

> If anything, I'm perhaps the only Dutch composer in Holland because I feel I'm out of Mondrian and Willem de Kooning. [Laughs.] I feel I'm out of that tradition, serious and experimental. [46]

Feldman got to know Mondrian's work before he met any of the Abstract Expressionists, even though he does not get the chronology quite right:

> The early Mondrian's were very important to me in terms of their asymmetric rhythm, and they were very important to a lot of painters. There was a big Mondrian show in 1950. Mondrian influenced me tremendously. [47]

There was, however, no Mondrian show in New York in 1950, but there was a big exhibition of his work at the Sidney Janis Gallery from 10 October – 12 November 1949, *Piet Mondrian, Paintings 1910 through 1944*, in which clear examples of paintings containing some form of a grid structure were shown: *Composition in Line* (1916/17), *Composition* 1916 (1916), and *Composition No.12: Composition with Blue* (1937-42).

There are two of Mondrian's paintings that are extremely clear examples of a very regular use of the grid (*Grid Composition 8, Checker Board, dark colours* and *Grid Composition* 9, *Checker Board, light colours* (both 1919), but these were not seen in New York until 1953 and 1957 respectively.[48] Of course there is no reason why Feldman could not have seen these as reproductions in a book or some other publication, but there is no known source for this information either way. The Museum of Modern Art at the time had a very small number of Mondrian's later works in their collection, the most telling example of a grid work being the *Broadway Boogie Woogie* (1942-43) which Feldman could very well have seen.

There is some circumstantial evidence for the link between Mondrian and the grid pieces, found in a letter written by Pierre Boulez to Cage in which Boulez expresses his very critical opinion on the grid scores Feldman sent to him. It is not entirely sure which ones Boulez saw, but they were in all probability *Intersection 1* and *2*:

> I am very sorry not to have much liked Morton Feldman's *Intersections*.
>
> As to Mondrian, no, I love him truly not at all. For his pictures are the most denuded of mystery that have ever been in the world. Let us distinguish all the same this false science from a true science which is less easy to decipher. It is against the facility of a Mondrian that I rise up. Such simple solutions are not to my taste. (Personally the abstract pictures of Klee, – and even the others – are infinitely closer to me and I find them much more probing, even in pictorial technique.) For the rest, genuine works are those in which one can never come to an end (infinite nucleus of the night); and when all is said, one has still said nothing, and one will never say anything.[49]

The whereabouts of the letter Feldman sent to Boulez is not known, so we don't know exactly what Feldman had to say about Mondrian, but it is clear that he cited the Dutch painter as an important influence or at least expressed his admiration for the work.

The other painter that Feldman acknowledges as a major influence on the graph pieces and specifically the way they are composed is Jackson Pollock (1912-1956).

At first sight, Feldman's claim that both Mondrian and Pollock have been major influences on his work may seem somewhat surprising – after all, their work could hardly be more different. However, Feldman understood very well that Mondrian had never been a methodical painter, but, as he said "felt his way" similarly to his own way of composing. There is an underlying similarity to Pollock's intuitive method of painting, even if the stylistic result ends up being miles apart. Feldman stressed often enough that he was not preoccupied with style, and he could recognize that there was a strong overlap in the way both painters worked. He would claim that Pollock's use of colour was influenced by the Dutch artist:

> The palette was influenced by Mondrian. If you take a look at those early paintings of Pollock, he would use the primary colours of Mondrian. [50]

In conversations with the Dutch painter Steven Aalders, it was pointed out to me that in fact Feldman was correct: if one studies Pollock's palette there is a strong preference for using reds, blues and yellows, in addition to black, white, silver (grey) plus a kind of taupe.

Clement Greenberg, in his 1967 article on Pollock, also make some very pertinent points on the two artists having more in common that one would realise at first sight:

> Like Mondrian, Pollock demonstrates that not skill or dexterity but inspiration, vision, intuitive decision, is what counts essentially in the creation of aesthetic quality.

> Inspiration declares itself in the overall conception of a work: the choosing, placing, and relating of what goes into it. [...] Again, like Mondrian, Pollock demonstrates that something related to skill is likewise unessential to the creation of aesthetic quality: namely, personal touch, individuality of execution, handwriting, 'signature'. [51]

Even though Feldman would undoubtedly have agreed with the main gist of Greenberg's argument, he would very probably have questioned his downplaying of the importance of skill. He would often lament the fact that his students are not interested in skill:

> But we have everything. I tell my students we're all Duchamp: we didn't invent major sixths, we didn't invent major and minor sevenths, we didn't invent the violin, we cannot build the forty-thousand-dollar Steinway, we cannot print the money to pay the Kronos and Aki Takahashi to play at the festival. So, there are many things that are already preinvented. All we have to do is to drive the car. However, many people feel that in art you don't have to know how to drive. [...] And they feel they don't have to know anything. So I went into my classroom the other day and I looked at them and I said "God forbid, if any of you get very sick, and you need an operation, I have the right person for you. They never studied medicine, but they love to cut up people, and they love the sight of blood, so let me recommend this person. They're very sincere. They believe that medicine should be free expression, and they feel they should be able to do it any way they want." I asked one student "what do you think it is all about in university?" He said, "I insist on my academic freedom."

> I said, "don't you know that in a university academic freedom is the freedom to be academic? [52]

The use of the grid is something Feldman went back to over and over again. Not only are the graph pieces, due to their particular notational device, totally reliant on a pre-notated grid, his later works, and the conventionally notated works from the 1950's is also written in a very strict grid matrix of usually nine bars in each system, regardless of the instrumentation of the piece. (Fig. 6)

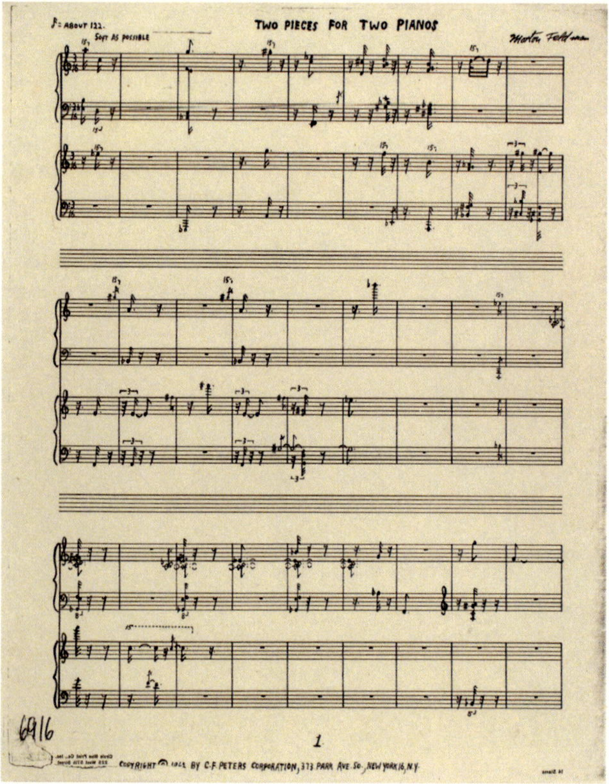

FIGURE 6

Morton Feldman, *Two Pieces for Two Pianos*, page 1 (1954).

This grid, however, often serves a different purpose. In the graph pieces each box or column of boxes represents one ictus, that is to say, one beat in a regular, unchanging tempo (although there could be an exception to this in *Ixion*). In the later works each bar looks similar in length but can be any length, within a steady tempo, as the metre can change per bar. The grid is visible, but often not audible in time, although it can be audible in content, where each 'box' (in this case 'bar') is a more or less self-contained musical unit. Feldman actually spoke about the problems of 'getting over the barline' in a talk about his piece *For Christian Wolff* in Darmstadt, 24 July 1986. In a few pieces, the best example being *Crippled Symmetry*, the grid structure is clearly visible on the page, but since all instruments have a different time content, the structure will be completely inaudible, and the music does in no way sound as it looks. (Fig. 7)

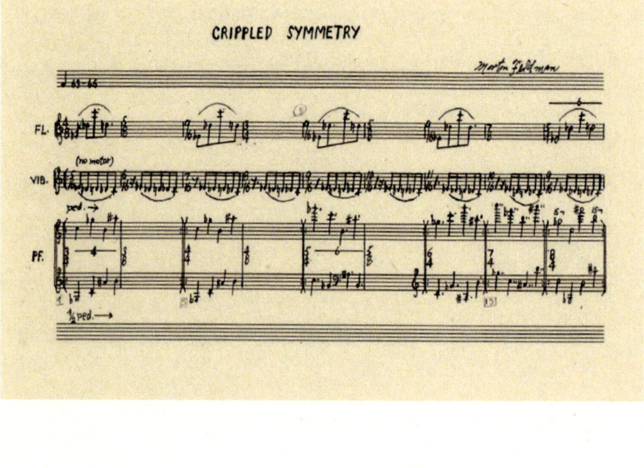

FIGURE 7

Morton Feldman, *Crippled Symmetry*, page 1, first system (1983).

When asked about his views on using the grid in his work Feldman said:

> It's still there. One of the problems I had with the early grid is that there was a tendency to be too design-oriented. It was easy to make wonderful designs on the page, which I did. [53]

It is certainly lamentable then that Feldman's grid-based but conventionally notated scores are now being typeset without any attempt to keep the visual grid structure intact and are no longer available in their original manuscript form. For pieces that in their concept rely so strongly on visual elements and on working with patterns not only in the music but on the written page as well, removing the grid structure means that the performer loses a very important layer of information that is vital for understanding the structure of the composition.

Graph scores or graphic scores?

The idea of changing aspects of standard Western musical notation to express musical or extra-musical ideas is not new. We see experiments with score design as far back as the 15th century with pieces notated in the shape of a cross, or heart, or chess board.

This notational tradition is, however, either a way of making the score look like the subject of the composition, see *Belle, Bonne, Sage* by the French Ars Subtilior composer Baude Cordier (c1380-c1440) (Fig. 8), or simply an interesting way to visualise the musical structure, as in the fascinating riddle canon *Ave Maris Stella* by the Dutch composer Ghiselin Danckerts (c1510-1567) (Fig. 9), in which the fragments of the canon are presented in the shape of a chess board, as a puzzle that needs to be solved before the piece can be performed.

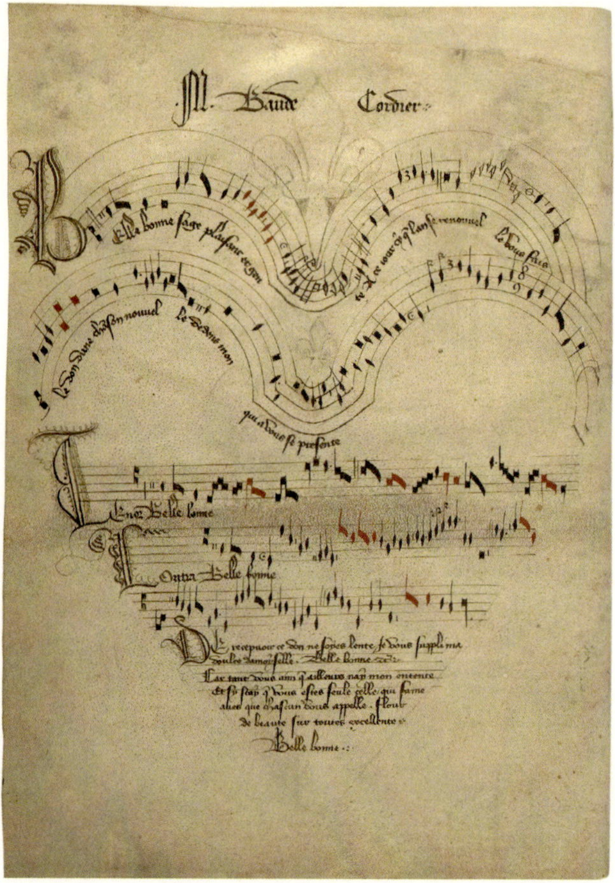

FIGURE 8

Baude Cordier, *Belle, Bonne, Sage,* date unknown.

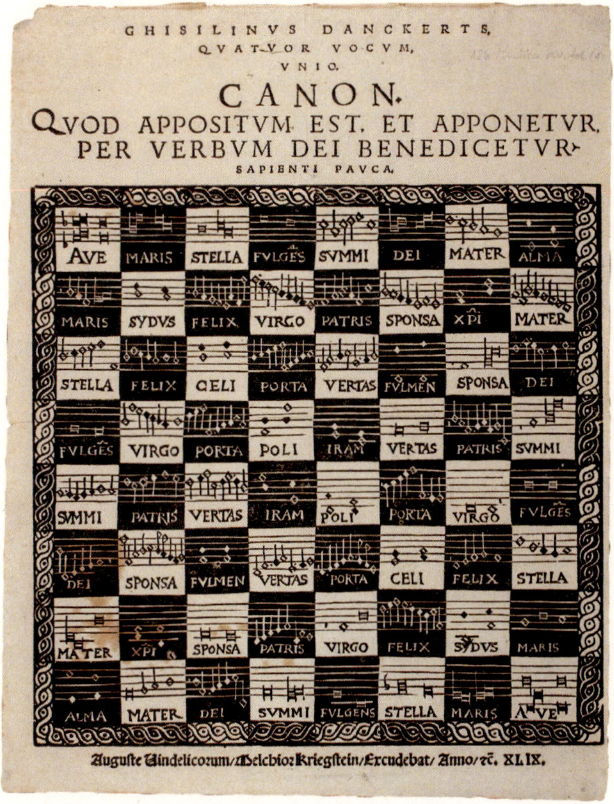

FIGURE 9

Ghiselin Danckerts, *Ave Maris Stella*, (1535).

Such scores are nevertheless traditional in their musical language and concept and the graphic novelty is just that, a fun way to notate. It has no bearing on the musical structure of the piece itself nor on its performance. It seems therefore that Feldman was the first composer to change the actual concept of standard Western notation and use non-standard signs and designs to be able to notate the specific kind of freedom he wanted to give to the performer. However, even though the idea of using different kinds of graphic information to notate music was taken up very quickly by other composers, and we see scores by Cage, Brown, Wolff and others from the early 1950s developing this idea, I would distinguish between the concepts of graphic scores and graph scores whereby one could make a case for graph scores being a specific subset of graphic scores. Feldman usually referred to the works as graph, not graphic and the differences lie in the idea of what was to be conveyed in notation.

In Feldman's graph scores the design uses the grid as a stand-in for the standard five-line system with the boxes functioning as either bars or beats to be filled with sounds. Most of the traditional function of notation is maintained: a regular succession of beats, often a tempo marking, a standard layout of the instrumentation, no use of any novel signs that might signify extended playing techniques, the music always moves from left to right, etc. Feldman's notation was therefore devised specifically to be able to notate the amount of freedom the performer would have but was not intended to give any flexibility to any other musical parameter.

In graphic scores such as produced by Cage, Brown and a whole host of other composers since the early 1950s, we can often see that standard signs are replaced, and special signs for non-standard playing techniques are invented or even totally replaced by text instructions only. The structure of such scores is often flexible or to be determined by the performer, tempo is most likely no longer given or replaced by a chronometric system and more often than not, a lot of thought would go into the visual design and the idea of the score as an aesthetically pleasing work, rather than Feldman's more utilitarian use of the graphic elements. In contrast Feldman would stick to the one kind of design he came up with and only slightly added some new elements to some of the later graph scores, but even these would be limited to very standard musical expressions such as repetitions, flutter-tonguing, or tremolo and would usually just consist of a letter or the mark that would be used in a traditional score.

The term 'graph score' seems to indicate the visual analogy to graphs and graph paper rather than alluding to graphic design. The graph structure is always hand drawn and Feldman did not use pre-printed graph paper in any of the graph scores. In fact, as I wrote earlier in this chapter, the early graph scores were notated in a non-too clear and imprecise manner, at least according to John Cage, and Cage took it upon himself to re-notate two of Feldman's scores to show how it should be done. We see that the score of *Projection 4* is entirely in Cage's handwriting save for the composer's name on the cover, and the same goes for *Intersection 2*.

I would conclude that the graphic elements of the graph scores were not invented therefore to fulfil a desire to come up with a whole new way of notating freedom of multiple parameters in as aesthetically pleasing a way as possible, but as a way to come to grips with ideas about not needing the prescribe pitches and rhythm in the traditional precise way that made logical sense to the composer and, secondarily, to the performer.

Ixion
History and Scores

In 1958, the choreographer Merce Cunningham asked Feldman to compose a score for a new dance piece that was to be premiered on 17th August of that year at the Eleventh American Dance Festival at the Connecticut College for Women in New London, Connecticut. The dance was eventually titled *Summerspace*, although Feldman's composition received the title *Ixion*.

Costumes and set were designed by Robert Rauschenberg, who decided to cover both the dancers and the stage backdrop with a series of pointillistic coloured dots, that effectively camouflaged the dancers when they were not in motion and made their bodies shimmer in front of the set when they moved around.

Merce Cunningham stated at the time:

> I'm trying to get two pieces done for this-here Festival. one with new work, a new intersection for orchestra by Morty. about 15 minutes long, seems to be doing with people and velocities, at least a hell of a lot is on the fast side, four girls and Remy and myself, I have the feeling it's like looking

> at part of an enormous landscape and you can only see the action in this particular portion of it. I hope it's dazzling rather than willy-nilly.[1]

Feldman worked on the score independently from both Cunningham and Rauschenberg, as was the normal modus operandi for Cunningham, only bringing together all elements at the last moment where both composer and choreographer would adhere to a time structure but would otherwise be free to do what they needed to without prior knowledge of each other's part. Even so, Feldman recalls that he had a telephone conversation with Rauschenberg:

> Bob told me that the set was pointillistic, and that he would use the same colours to paint the costumes. That gave me an idea also: rather than having three scenes going – Merce, Bob, and myself – I decided to melt into the décor. So the score is pointillistic. [...] And so it's not a characteristic score of mine. But the ballet looks very beautiful, just perfect, like you get a little speck in your eye and you wipe it away. It makes it even more frontal because you are having all this thing, vibrating there, and then out in front there's the band going. And it wasn't until the dress rehearsal that I actually saw what was going on.[2]

The title of the piece, *Ixion*, comes from Greek mythology. Feldman refers to it in the WBAI conversation with Cage on 16 January 1967:

> Do you know that marvellous myth of Ixion? In a sense, I was aware of that when I wrote "Ixion" for "Summerspace". Where this man has a beautiful horse, and he didn't want

anybody to steal it – this is one of the myths of Ixion. So, he decided that he wasn't going to give it a name. Zeus saw the horse and stole it. So, Ixion ran all over the place, looking for the horse, but he couldn't call it; you see (laughs), it had no name. That's the basis of the story. Ixion got involved in other adventures, but that's the basis of the story. And there's something about not being in the world, where what you do is not named.[3]

The story Feldman alludes to is not part of any known version of the Ixion myth. There are some links with horses, in that his relation Eioneus seized Ixion's horses as security, leading to Eioneus' murder by Ixion. He later tried to rape Hera, but Zeus put a cloud in her place, which was impregnated by Ixion, resulting in the birth of the first Centaurs, half man, half horse.[4] The story is also not part of any other Greek myth that I have been able to track down and it is unknown to me what the original source of this story could be.

The Scores

Ixion has two versions, both of which can be used for performance, with or without the dance. The first version, which hereafter is called the ensemble version is scored for 3 flutes, clarinet, horn, trumpet, trombone, piano, 3-7 cellos, and 2-4 double basses, making a total of 13 to 19 performers. The published version of his score is written on 17 pages[5] (excluding the single page of performance instructions) each containing one system with a grid of 10 layers of 40 boxes, where each box is one ictus, except for the last page, which contains only 25 boxes, making the total length of the piece 745 boxes. (Fig. 10)

There are separate boxes for each of the three flutes, but only one for the 3-7 cellos, and one for the 2-4 double basses, who will therefore all have to read from the same part. Each box contains either a number between 1 and 24 or is left empty. If a number is present, this indicates the amount of sounds to be played on or within the box. If no number is present, the amount of sounds is understood to be zero, and therefore this box will remain silent.

Ixion does not follow the notional rules of many of Feldman's earlier graph pieces, where each instrument would have 3 layers of boxes, indicating that the sounds should be in the high, middle, or low register of the instrument. Instead, each instrument only has one single layer of boxes, and the performance instructions say that the piece:

> is to be played in the high registers of the instruments except for a brief section in which the low registers are indicated.[6]

This section can be found on page 9 of the scores, starting at the last 4 boxes, and lasting until box 21 on page 10, making the low sounding section of the piece 25 boxes in length, being a mere 3.35% of the overall length of the piece. The same idea is used in *Atlantis* (1959), but here the low section is only 5 boxes in length, or 0.67% of the piece, although in this piece the piano part is the exception and does follow the high, middle, low notation.

To make it easier for the performers to find their way in the score and/or part, the piece has been numbered in units of 10 boxes. These are indicated with roman numerals at the end of each section of 10, I to V, with the next section numbering I^1 to V^1, I^2 to V^2, and so on, until the last section, which should have been numbered I^{14} to IV^{14}, except that Feldman forgot to write in the III and IV, leaving only the ^{14}'s.

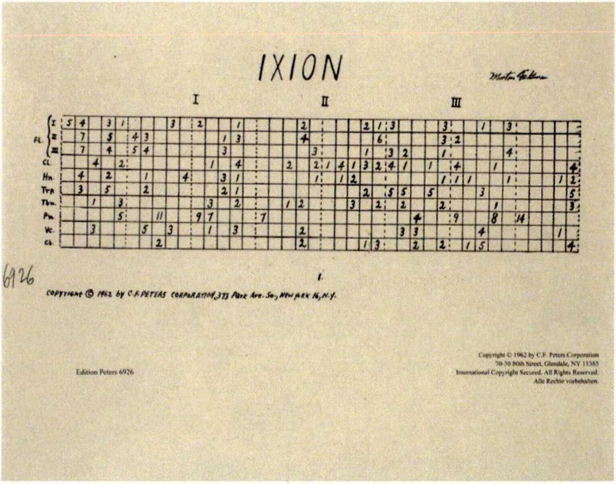

FIGURE 10

Morton Feldman, *Ixion*, ensemble version, page 1 (1958).

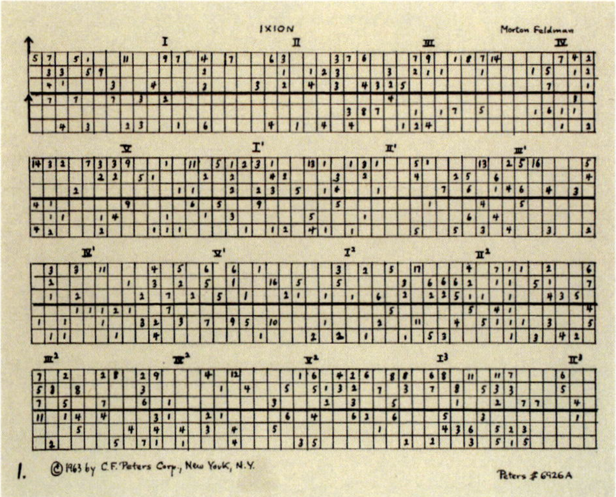

FIGURE 11

Morton Feldman, *Ixion*, 2-piano version, page 1 (1958).

The second version is scored for 2 pianos (and is henceforth referred to as the 2-piano version), which makes it likely that it was meant initially as a piano reduction, making it possible for the dancers to rehearse without needing to have the whole ensemble present. It might also have been a way of making it possible to perform the work in smaller venues, where the space to accommodate the 13-19 players (including a grand piano) was unavailable, but with enough room to accommodate two pianos, or it may simply have been a solution for financially tight productions. It would probably have been all of these reasons, and the performance history of *Summerspace* includes performances with both the ensemble and the 2-piano version. It is interesting to note that the Cunningham Dance Company, aside from a few very early performances for which there are no video or audio recordings always performed the dance with the 2-piano version. Performances with the ensemble version have been done by other companies, notably the Juilliard School in 2009 and the New York City Ballet in 2019.[7]

This version is notated over 5 pages, with 4 systems on pages 1 to 4, and 2 systems on page 5 (Fig. 11). These systems have 6 layers of 43 boxes, again each one being one ictus, 3 for each piano, on the first page, and 6 layers of 42 boxes on pages 2, 3 and 4. Page 5 has only 2 systems, one of 42 boxes and one of 25 boxes in length, giving the piece a total length of 746 boxes, which means there is a discrepancy between the two versions, where the 2-piano version is 1 box longer.

After doing some careful searching, it transpires that Feldman made one counting error. As in the ensemble version, the score is divided into sections of 10 boxes, with the same method of numbering. However, section III[7] is not 10 but 11 boxes in length. The extra box is the second box of this section, which is empty for all voices. It is the first box after the brief low passage of the piece, which might account for the confusion in counting. Also, the difference in layout will possibly have attributed to the error: the ensemble version has dotted vertical lines demarcating subsections of 5 boxes (although Feldman forgot the one between III^8 and IV^8, which instead is a non-dotted line), whereas the 2-piano version does not have this notational feature, making it potentially more difficult to keep one's bearings. All this means that when performing the 2-piano version one has to make a decision on whether the score needs to be presented as is, or corrected to make up for the discrepancy. I would opt for a correction of the score, leaving out the empty extra box, but if one wants to see the 2-piano version as a completely separate piece, not a mere reduction of the ensemble version, one could of course choose to leave it in. (Fig. 12)

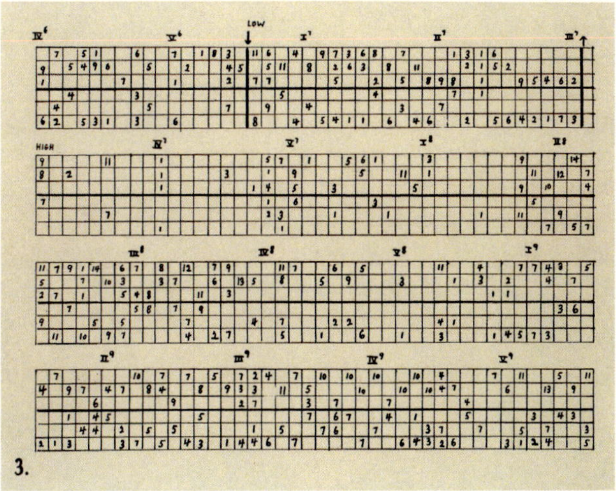

FIGURE 12

Morton Feldman, *Ixion*, 2-piano version, page 3 (1958).

The extra box is the last one in the first system.

There are some other difficulties with this version, which could hinder in preparing an accurate performance. The performance instructions that are included with the 2-piano version are identical to the one in the ensemble version. Whether this is because Feldman did not see the need for a specific set of instructions, which might point to its use as a rehearsal score only, or because the publisher, for whatever reason, chose not to include the correct one with the score, it makes some aspects of the performance less than straightforward.

There is a separate set of instructions that was given to David Tudor, but this has never been part of the published material. The other big problem that must be solved, and which might have been clarified with a rewritten set of performance instructions, is the notation of this version. As mentioned, the 2-piano version has both pianos written as a set of 3 layers of boxes. This in itself is wholly consistent with the way the other graph pieces for one or two pianos are notated: *Projection 2 for Two Pianos* (1951), *Intersection 2* (1951), and *Intersection 3* (1953), where the layers would stand for high, middle and low register sounds, but since the instructions are very clear that the whole piece is to be performed in the high register, with exception of the 25 boxes indicated "low", the function of the 3 layers is suddenly very problematic. One could speculate that the performers need to divide the high register of the piano into 'high-high', 'middle-high' and 'low-high', as indeed the separate instructions given to Tudor specify, but often this does not seem to correlate with the way the numbers are transferred from the ensemble score into the 2-piano score.

The score of *Ixion* had to be collapsed from 10 to 6 layers, making it necessary to condense the material to take into account the technical possibilities of the pianists. This poses several problems: a way has to be found to reduce, or combine, the material in the original version from 10 to 6, without losing too much musical or visual information. If we look at the way the score was reduced in musical terms, we need to look at two things: the vertical alignment of the numbers in the boxes, and the total number of sounds per ictus.

In any traditional piano reduction, we would necessarily see that not all the information present in the full score would find its way into the piano version, as practical and physical limitations are different for one or two pianists compared to an ensemble or orchestra. It is the decision of the arranger to make sure the most vital information is retained, and as little as possible is thrown away. In *Ixion,* however, these decisions are a lot less clear-cut. Even though a lot of the piece consists of relatively empty areas where only a handful of instruments play, making it straightforward enough to bring down from 10 to 6 layers, the fuller parts of the score are the ones where a conscious decision needs to be made. In large parts of the piece, it is clear that where an ictus has a lot of information, and the total number of sounds per ictus is more than would comfortably be performable by four hands on two pianos, the number of sounds in the 2-piano version would need to be (sometimes considerably) reduced.

It is quite difficult to make any sensible comment about how Feldman reached the decisions he made. It seems that a lot of the choices were made quite intuitively with a rather broad-brush stroke. It can be safely assumed Feldman either worked on both versions simultaneously or wrote the 2-piano version very soon after completing the ensemble version. The latter is dated in the score 'August 1958' but the former is not dated. However, as we know that Cage and Tudor made a recording of the 2-piano version very probably in October 1958, Feldman would have to have made the 2-piano version by then. There is an issue though in that the recording is not of the complete piece and ends at the end of the first system of page 3. Whether this was because Feldman had not yet finished the 2-piano version or because of some other decision is unclear. In addition, the blueprint copy in the collection of the Paul Sacher Stiftung has the same size and layout as the published 2-piano score, contrary to the manuscript of the ensemble version, which differs substantially from the published version. This could indicate that the 2-piano version was made immediately after the ensemble version was completed and would be an indication that no specific version-related decisions were made with regards to the overall visual structure of the piece.

Another set of decisions that would need to be made is on how to deal with the specific instrumentation of the ensemble version. This links in directly with the division of each of the parts for the two pianos into 3 layers. The ensemble score calls for instruments that have different pitch sets: a flute will necessarily be higher in pitch, especially when instructed to play in the high register, than a trombone or a double bass. This would necessitate the placement of the numbers for higher-pitched instruments on the top layer, for middle-pitched instruments on the middle layer, and for low-pitched instruments on the low layer of the piano reduction, at least if we see the 3 layers as high-high, middle-high, and low-high, as I have proposed earlier (and as Feldman's instructions to Tudor confirm). We can see that for quite a lot of the piece this seems to be more or less adhered to, but definitely not in a consistent manner.

In order, to try and find out what kind of relationship there is between the two versions I have made a comparative analysis of the scores. A difference in the number of sounds in itself would not say much about whether the 2-piano version is a re-composition or a piano reduction. It is quite customary for piano reductions to be exactly that: a reduction, in which for playability's sake not all material from the orchestral score is included, but as much as is performable without sacrificing both the character and the main musical material. For *Ixion* it is not quite that simple; even though it is evident that Feldman kept the overall character of the piece similar, if not identical, the nature of the composition makes it more or less an irrelevant exercise to try and determine if there is anything in the score that could be seen as main musical material.

A number of decisions had to be made in order to make a comparison possible. For each instrument in the ensemble version a relative register had to be chosen, high high, middle high, or low high (with their counterpart's high low, middle low, and low low for the short passage where low register is indicated). This in itself could very much be open to interpretation and discussion, but in the end, I decided on the following:

Flute 1, 2 & 3: high high (HH), high low (HL)
Clarinet: middle high (MH), high low (HL)
Horn: low high (LH), middle low (ML)
Trumpet: middle high (MH), high low (HL)
Trombone: low high (LH), middle low (ML)
Piano: high high, middle high, low high (HH, MH, LH), high low, middle low, low low (HL, ML, LL)
Cellos: low high (LH), middle low (ML)
Double Basses: low high (LH), low low (LL)

For each box (ictus) I then compared the total number of sounds, noting if the 2-piano version had the same, more or fewer sounds. Then I compared the distribution of sounds over the three registers to try and find out if and how the decisions on changes in register could have been made. The complete analysis can be found in Chapter 3.

The ensemble version has a grand total of 9,831 sounds, and the 2-piano version 8,112, resulting in a discrepancy of 1,719, making the 2-piano version contain 80.39% of the amount of sounds the ensemble version has. Only the section between II^{12} and I^{13} sees more sounds in the 2-piano version, corresponding with the two pages in the score where all boxes for all instruments in the ensemble version contain the figure 1 (barring the empty boxes and two one-box interludes). Forty-one boxes have more sounds in the 2-piano version, 461 have the same amount of sounds in both versions, and 243 have more sounds in the ensemble version. In percentages this is 5.50%, 61.88% and 32.62%, respectively. Then there is the one extra empty ictus which for this analysis will not be counted. We can say that there is a sizeable minority of the piece where the two versions differ, but the overall pointillistic character Feldman was after is not affected.

When comparing the version with regards to the amount of discrepancy in register, we need to recognise the problems identified above with regards to determining which instruments are set in which part of the overall range. In the analysis I have therefore consistently used the word 'possibly' (poss.) where a purely personal decision needed to be made. Of the 745 boxes that make up the score (excluding the one extra box in the 2-piano version) we find that 261 have no changes in register (this includes the empty boxes, of which there are 70 in the ensemble version and 71 in the 2-piano version), and 484 have sounds that possibly shifted in register, or 35.03% and 64.97%.

Even though it is quite clear when listening to both versions that the overall character and musical identity of the piece is the same, there is one passage that initially seems clearly different, both visually and aurally: the passage between II^{12} and I^{13} is unique in the ensemble version for containing the number 1 for each instrument in most of the boxes. This makes the passage very uniform in density compared with the rest of the piece. The 2-piano version, however, does not have this characteristic, and although the number of sounds in each of these boxes is the same, namely 13 (with exception of the first, which has 8 sounds), the distribution of the 13 sounds is different with each iteration, both in register and in number of sounds per piano. Even though this may at first glance look like a very different compositional decision, if we consider the nature of the piece, where each player needs to decide per box which sounds to play, and where in the box to place them, then this difference falls away. The passage can sound similar in both versions. As a counterargument one could point to the existing recording of the ensemble version of *Ixion*,[8] where this passage is performed by all players starting and finishing their sounds simultaneously, filling the total length of the box, but I would say that this is a (possibly non-intentional) misinterpretation, or at least a limited interpretation of the instructions. This is explored in more detail in chapter 4, Ixion - Performance Issues.

The choices made for the specific distribution of the sounds over the 3 layers of both pianos (6 layers in total) is anything but straightforward. Partly because it seems that Feldman did not try to be very strict and allowed himself a lot of freedom to determine how many sounds should go in which piano and in which particular layer – sometimes numbers are transposed one-on-one, sometimes divided up between the pianos – partly because care has to be taken that the piano parts remain playable, so larger numbers need to be reduced or redistributed. Also, due to the fact, except for the piano, all instruments used in *Ixion* do not really have a fixed top note. This depends on the performer and their abilities. Especially with string players it is possible to play extremely high notes, on cellos and double basses by using artificial harmonics, something that, by not being mentioned at all in the performance instructions, would be implicitly allowed. This makes determining whether an instrument would be seen as high-high, middle-high, or low-high an almost arbitrary decision. One could safely assume that a double bass would be low-high, but even so, it could go up above the top notes of a horn and a trombone, especially when using harmonics. A trumpet might normally have an accepted upper limit, but there are a lot of players who specialise in the higher register and can easily go far beyond this. In short, most instruments could fall in more than one category. Even so, Feldman clearly indicates that all notes (except the one short, low fragment) must be in the high register, which would imply that performers would have to choose sounds that are indeed in what they perceive as the upper part of their range.

Determining the bottom of the high register is also a highly personal choice. Is it the highest octave, the two highest octaves, the highest one-third of the range, can it be a flexible limit? All these decisions are up to the performer. If we look at the version of the 2-piano version of *Ixion* that David Tudor prepared for his performances,[9] we see that he took middle c as the lowest note (as per Feldman's own instructions), meaning that the high register would be more or less the upper half of the piano (the top 49 out of 88 keys, or the top 46 out of 85 for older model pianos going up to A''''), but in his written out versions of *Intersection 2* and *Intersection 3* we see that the boundaries of the ranges are somewhat flexible, and notes can be in both lower and middle register, or in both middle and high register.[10] The decisions seem not to have any rule-based system behind them, and might be taken purely intuitively. All this makes it very difficult to ascertain with any kind of certainty if the choices Feldman made when transposing the ensemble version to the 2-piano version were made by trying to map the various ranges of the instruments onto the pianos, whether the decisions would be practical with regards to playability, or if decisions were made analogous to those in the ensemble version, where they would be visual as much as musical.

I have chosen three fragments from both versions of *Ixion* to attempt to gain a more detailed, in-depth look at the differences between the versions. The first excerpt is the beginning of the piece, being the first page in the ensemble version, or the first 40 boxes or icti.

In these 40 icti we see that 12 are without any problems; the numbers add up, and the registers are equivalent in both versions. The others have inconsistencies of various kinds. 9 icti have fewer sounds in the 2-piano version, but 2 actually have more: 1 has 3, and 1 has 5 more sounds than the ensemble version. 1 ictus (number 13, or the third ictus of I) is completely empty in the 2-piano version, even though there are 9 sounds in the ensemble version. It could well be that this is a simple mistake on Feldman's part, and he forgot to put numbers in, but this is impossible to find out for certain, as (at least to my knowledge) there are no sketches or other materials that would provide extra information. There is one other ictus in the piece that contains sounds in the ensemble version, but not in the 2-piano version: the fourth ictus of III^2. All other icti in the piece have either sounds in both versions, or no sounds in both versions, the only exception being the extra ictus in the 2-piano version (the second in III^7), which does not exist in the ensemble version.

Looking at the icti with possible changes in register, of which there are 18 in this section, it is often difficult to say what the rationale behind the change was. Sometimes it could be just a small variation, where one of the clarinet sounds goes to another layer (LH instead of MH, as seen in the third ictus of the piece), sometimes all the sounds shift register (ictus 6, where 9 sounds in the second and third flute are set to MH in piano 1), and more often than not, the change could very well be explained by an instrument straddling 2 layers – a cello could easily be MH and LH, or even HH when using harmonics, and a clarinet could be MH and LH.

To try and find out if this amount of discrepancy would be present in other parts of the score, I have made a similar inventory of two other excerpts of equal length: from IV^8 until and including II^9, and the final 40 icti (from V^{13} 6th ictus to the end).

In the second excerpt, which is in general a rather sparse section of the score, we nonetheless see a fairly large degree of incongruency: out of 40, only 13 icti are without changes (7 of which are totally empty, and therefore have no information that would be subject to change), 8 have fewer sounds in the 2-piano version, none have fewer notes in the ensemble version, and 24 have possible changes in register.

The final section also sees a large amount of change. This is for a large part due to it being the densest part of the piece, and we can safely say that Feldman was working towards an ever-increasing density, with the final ictus having the largest number of sounds in the entire composition (101). It will be hardly or even not at all possible to fit all the information of this section into 2 piano parts, and the comparison reveals that only 7 icti have the same amount of sounds in both versions, 31 have fewer sounds in the 2-piano version; still, 1 ictus has 1 fewer sound in the ensemble version (10th of V^{13}, with 11 sounds in the 2-piano version against 10 in the ensemble version). 26 icti have possible shifts in register.

After going through the whole analysis, it has become clear to me that nowhere in the piece it can be said unequivocally that Feldman used some kind of direct transcription from the ensemble version to form the 2-piano version. There are boxes where a one-on-one transfer is evident, especially where the texture is very thin, where there is only a single instrument playing, or where there are no sounds at all, but even in these cases there are exceptions. The overall density of the composition is generally adhered to, so it is safe to say that the overall structure is the same, but that within this structure the precise content of the boxes was determined with what seems a large amount of freedom, more intuitively than with any kind of rule-based system serving as a base. This would be totally in line with what Feldman and Christian Wolff said about the limited usefulness of analysing his music by trying to find any kind of system[11], or Feldman's remark to Han Reiziger in the 1985 radio interview:

> But I do have a system, and my system essentially is thought.[12]

What we can say with some certainty is that the actual instrumentation has not been considered, and there does not seem to be any rules as to which instruments go into which piano or even in which part of the register. I would suspect that most of the decision-making process would have focused on balancing density between the pianos and making sure the overall sounding result would be somewhat similar between the two versions, at least from a formal point of view.

After looking at the two versions in detail and after completing the comparative analysis, I conclude that the two versions of *Ixion* cannot be seen simply as an ensemble piece and its piano reduction, but can be regarded as separate works, albeit coming from the same basic idea and structure.

The similarities are numerous, but so are the differences, and furthermore, performances of the two versions can in my experience sound very different, to the extent that it is unlikely to hear one version and be reminded of the other, or even recognise them as being the same piece.

One possible additional reason for the many discrepancies could be that the compositional process of *Ixion* was not purely a musical one but was to a large degree based on visual considerations. This might have influenced the distribution of the sounds over the layers to quite a substantial degree and the visual might well have been equally important or even have trumped the aural. In addition, the 2-piano version seems to have been written making use of a different kind of score design: where the ensemble version was done using separate strips cut from a writing pad, the 2-piano version looks to have been notated directly onto the 2-system grid structure we see in the published version. This leads me to believe that the 2-piano version was made using the ensemble score as a model, and not with the same level of attention to the visual aspect of the score, which would have made it more of a proper piano reduction. Still, the differences are numerous and important enough to conclude that the 2-piano version transcends a mere reduction. The way the piece may have been specifically influenced by Jackson Pollock's painting technique is elaborated upon in Chapter 5, Ixion and Jackson Pollock.

Comparative Analysis

Rehearsal nr.	Ictus	Inst.	HH	MH	LH	Total	Inst.	HH	MH	LH	Total	Discrepancies
	1	F1:5	5			5	P1	5			5	none
	2	F1:4 F2:7 F3:7 Hn:4 Tp:3	18	3	4	25	P1 P2	7 7	3	4	21	Missing: 4 (f1HH)
	3	Cl:4 Tb:1 Vc:3		4	4	8	P1 P2		3	1 4	8	Poss: 1LH instead MH
	4	F1:3 F2:5 F3:4 Hn:2 Tp:5	12	5	2	19	P1 P2	5 7			12	Missing: 5MH 2LH
	5	F1:1 Cl:2 Tb:3 Pf:5	1 5	2 →	3 →	11	P1 P2	1	5	3	9	Missing; 2MH Pf is MH
	6	F2:4 F3:5	9			9	P1		9		9	Poss: 9 MH instead of HH
	7	F2:3 F3:4 Hn:1 Tp:2 Vc:5	7	2	6	15	P1 P2	7		3	10	Missing: 2MH 3LH
	8	Pf:11 Db:2	11	→	→ 2	13	P1 P2	11		2	13	none
	9	F1:3 Vc:3	3		3	6	P2	3		3	6	none
	10	Hn:4			4	4	P1			4	4	none
I	11	F1:2 Pf:9	2 9	→	→	11	P1 P2	9 2			11	none
	12	Cl:1 Tb:3 Pf:7 Vc:1	7	→ 1	→ 4	12	P1 P2	7		1	8	Missing: 1MH, 3LH
	13	F2:1 F3:3 Hn:3 Tp:2	4	2	3	9	P1 P2				0	Missing: 4HH, 2MH, 3LH
	14	F1:1 F2:3 Cl:4 Hn:1 Tp:1 Tb:2 Vc:3	4	5	6	15	P1 P2	4	2	3 6	15	Poss: 3LH instead MH
	15	Empty				0	Empty				0	none
	16	Pf:7	7	→	→	7	P1	7			7	none

Rehearsal nr.	Ictus	Inst.	HH	MH	LH	Total	Inst.	HH	MH	LH	Total	Discrepancies
	17	Empty				0	Empty				0	none
	18	Cl:2 Tb:1		2	1	3	P1			3	3	Poss: 2LH instead MH
	19	Fl1:2 Fl2:4 Tb:2 Vc:2 Db:2	4		6	10	P1 P2	6		 4	10	Poss: 2LH instead HH
	20	F3:3 Cl:2 Hn:1	3	2	1	6	P1	3	1	2	6	Poss: 1 MH instead LH
II	21	Cl:1		1		1	P2			1	1	Poss: 1 LH instead MH
	22	Cl:4 Hn:1		4	1	5	P1		1	4	5	Poss: 3LH instead MH
	23	Cl:1 Hn:2 Tb:3		1	5	6	P1 P2		2	 4	6	Poss: 1 MH instead LH
	24	F1:2 F3:1 Cl:3 Tp:2 Db:1	3	5	1	9	P1	3	3	3	9	Poss: 2 LH instead MH
	25	F1:1 F2:6 Cl:2 Tb:2 Db:3	7	2	5	14	P1 P2	7	 3	 4	14	Poss: 1 LH instead MH
	26	F1:3 F3:3 Cl:4 Tp:5	6	9		15	P1 P2	6	 8	4	18	Extra: 3 LH, Poss 1 LH instead MH
	27	F3:2 Cl:1 Tp:5 Tb:2 Vc:3	2	6	5	13	P1 P2		 7	3	10	Missing: 2 HH, 1 LH, Poss: 1 MH instead LH
	28	Pf:4 Vc:3 Db:2	4	→	→ 5	9	P1 P2	 4	3	2	9	Poss: 3 MH instead LH
	29	Cl:1 Tp:5		6		6	P1 P2			5 1	6	Poss: 6LH instead LH
	30	F1:3 F2:3 F3:1 Hn:1 Tb:2 Db:2	7		5	12	P1 P2	7	2 1	 2	12	Poss: 3MH instead LH

Rehear-sal nr.	Ictus	Inst.	HH	MH	LH	Total	Inst.	HH	MH	LH	Total	Discrepancies
III	31	F2:2 CL;4 Hn:1 Pf:9	9 2	→ 4	→ 1	16	P1 P2	9	1	 4	14	Missing: 2HH Poss: 3MH instead LH
	32	Hn:1 Db:1			2	2	P1 P2		1 1		2	Poss: MH instead LH
	33	F1:1 Tp:3 Vc:4 Db:5	1	3	9	13	P1 P2	1	 7		8	Missing: 5 LH Poss:4 MH instead LH
	34	Cl:1 Tb:1 Pf:8	8	→ 1	→ 1	10	P1	8			8	Missing: 1 MH, 1 LH
	35	F1:3 F3:4 Hn:1	7		1	8	P1 P2	7	1 5		13	Extra: 5 LH Poss: 1MH instead LH
	36	Pf:14	14	→	→	14	P1	14			14	none
	37	Empty				0	Empty				0	none
	38	Empty				0	Empty				0	none
	39	Hn:1 Vc:1			2	2	P1 P2		1 1		2	Poss: MH instead LH
	40	Cl:4 Hn:2 Tp:5 Tb:3 Db:4		9	9	18	P1 P2		5 6	7	18	Poss: 2 MH instead LH

Discrepancies Page 1:

12 icti none
9 icti with fewer numbers in 2-piano version
2 icti with fewer numbers in ensemble version
1 ictus empty in 2-piano version, but not in ensemble version
18 icti with numbers shifted in range.

Rehearsal nr.	Ictus	Inst.	HH	MH	LH	Total	Inst.	HH	MH	LH	Total	Discrep.
IV	1	Fl 1:7 Vc:2	7		2	9	Pf1 Pf2	7	 1	 1	9	Poss: 1MH instead LH
	2	Fl2:4 Fl3:3 Hn:1 Tp:1	7	1	1	9	Pf1 Pf2	4 3	1 1		9	Poss: 1MH instead LH
	3	Fl:2 Cl:1 Hn:2 Tb:2	2	1→	→ 4	7	Pf1 Pf2	2	2	1 2	7	Poss: 1MH instead LH
	4	Tp:4 Tb:3 Pf:14 Db:1	14→	→ 4	→ 4	22	Pf1 Pf2	14 4		 4	22	Poss: 1HH instead MH
	5	Fl1:1 Cl:2 Tp:1 Pf:3	3→ 1	→ 3	→	7	Pf1 Pf2	3 1	 1	 2	7	Poss: 2LH instead MH
	6	Fl1:2 Db:1	2		1	3	Pf1 Pf2	2	 1		3	Poss: 1MH instead LH
	7	Cl:1 Tb:1		1	1	2	Pf1			2	2	Poss: 1LH instead MH
	8	Pf:7	7→	→	→	7	Pf1	7			7	none
	9	Hn:3 Tb:2 Pf:3	3→	→	→ 5	8	Pf1 Pf2	3	2 1	 2	8	Poss: 3MH instead LH
	10	Fl2:3 Fl3:2 Tp:4	5	4		9	Pf1 Pf2	3	2 4		9	Poss: 2MH instead HH
V	11	Fl2:4 Fl3:5 Cl:4 Pf:9 Vc:3	9→ 9	→ 4	→ 3	26	Pf1 Pf2	9 9			18	Missing: 4MH, 3LH
	12	Fl1:3 Hn:2	3		2	5	Pf1		5		5	Poss: 3MH instead HH
	13	Hn:1 Db:1			2	2	Pf1 Pf2		1	 1	2	Poss: 1MH instead LH
	14	Pf:1 Db:1	1→	→	→ 1	2	Pf1 Pf2	1	 1	 1	3	Extra: 1MH
	15	Cl:1 Db:1		1	1	2	Pf1 Pf2			1 1	2	Poss: 1LH instead MH
	16	Fl1:2 Fl3:4 Hn:2 Tb:1 Pf:11 Vc:4	11→ 6	→	→ 7	24	Pf1 Pf2	11 6		1	18	Missing: 6LH
	17	Fl2:1 Tp:2	1	2		3	Pf1 Pf2		2 1		3	Poss: 1MH instead HH

Rehearsal nr.	Ictus	Inst.	HH	MH	LH	Total	Inst.	HH	MH	LH	Total	Discrep.
	18	Fl1:5 Fl3:5	10			10	Pf1 Pf2	5 5			10	none
	19	Fl2:3 Fl3:2 Cl:2 Tp:1	5	3		8	Pf1 Pf2	1	2 3	2	8	Poss: 2MH instead HH, 2LH instead HH
	20	Fl1:2 Cl:1	2	1		3	Pf1 Pf2	2		 1	3	Poss: 1LH instead MH
I[1]	21	Fl1:3 Cl:2 Pf:9	9→ 3	→ 2	→	14	Pf1 Pf2	3 9		2	14	Poss: 2LH instead MH
	22	Fl1:1 Cl:1 Tp:4 Db:3	1	5	3	9	Pf1 Pf2	1	4	3 1	9	Poss: 1LH instead MH
	23	Hn:2 Tp:2		2	2	4	Pf1 Pf2		2	 2	4	none
	24	Cl:2 Tb:3		2	3	5	Pf1			5	5	Poss: 2LH instead MH
	25	Fl1:4 Fl2:5 Fl3:4 Hn:6 Tp:5 Vc:2 Db:2	13	5	10	28	Pf1 Pf2	13	 5	 4	22	Missing: 6LH
	26	Fl1:1 Tb:1 Db:1	1		2	3	Pf1 Pf2	1		1 1	3	none
	27	Cl:4 Tp:1 Pf:5 Vc:2	5→	→ 5	→ 2	12	Pf1 Pf2	 5	3	4	12	Poss: 2LH instead MH
	28	Fl2:1 Hn:1	1		1	2	Pf1 Pf2	1		 1	2	none
	29	Fl1:3 Tp:3	3	3		6	Pf1 Pf2	3	2 1		6	none
	30	Fl2:1 Hn:1	1		1	2	Pf1	1		1	2	none
II[1]	31	Empty				0	Empty					none
	32	Empty				0	Empty					none
	33	Fl1:4 Hn:3 Tp:2 Tb:4 Pf:1	1→ 4	→ 2	→ 7	14	Pf1 Pf2	5	4	 5	14	Poss: 2MH instead LH
	34	Fl2:1 Pf:1	1→ 1	→	→	2	Pf1 Pf2	1 1			2	none
	35	Cl:5 Tb:2		5	2	7	Pf1			7	7	Poss: 5LH instead MH

Rehearsal nr.	Ictus	Inst.	HH	MH	LH	Total	Inst.	HH	MH	LH	Total	Discrep.
	36	Cl:2 Tp:1 Tb:4		3	4	7	Pf1 Pf2		2	 5	7	Poss: 1LH instead MH
	37	Fl2:3 Fl3:2 Cl:5 Hn:1 Tp:5 Tb:1	5	10	2	17	Pf1 Pf2		5 6	6	17	Poss: 1MH instead HH, 4LH instead HH
	38	Fl1:1 Fl2:5 Fl3:6 Cl:3 Hn:3 Tp:2 Tb:1 Pf:13	13→ 12	→ 5	→ 4	34	Pf1 Pf2	13 4		 3	20	Missing: 8HH, 5MH, 1LH
	39	Fl1:2 Fl2:1 Fl3:3 Cl:1 Tp:4	6	5		11	Pf1 Pf2		6 4	1	11	Poss: 5MH instead HH, 1LH instead HH
	40	Hn:2 Tp:3 Tb:5		3	7	10	Pf1 Pf2	2		4 4	10	Poss: 2MH instead HH, 1LH instead MH

Discrepancies Page 2:

10 icti none
4 icti with fewer numbers in 2-piano version
1 ictus with fewer numbers in ensemble version
0 icti empty in 2-piano version, but not in ensemble version
25 icti with numbers shifted in range.

Rehearsal nr.	Ictus	Inst.	HH	MH	LH	Total	Inst.	HH	MH	LH	Total	Discrep.
III[1]	1	Fl1:3 Fl3:6 Cl:6 Pf:1	1→ 9	→ 6	→	16	Pf1 Pf2	5 5		6	16	Poss: 6LH instead MH
	2	Pf:16	16→	→	→	16	Pf1	16			16	none
	3	Cl:7		7		7	Pf1 Pf2			4 3	7	Poss: 7LH instead MH
	4	Empty				0	Empty				0	none
	5	Cl:3		3		3	Pf1			3		Poss: 3LH instead MH
	6	Fl1:5 Tp:6	5	6		11	Pf1 Pf2	5	4	 2	11	Poss: 2LH instead MH
	7	Tp:1		1		1	Pf2		1		1	none
	8	Fl2:3 Hn:1 Tp:2 Db:1	3	2	2	7	Pf1 Pf2	3	2	1 1	7	none
	9	Cl:1 Hn:1		1	1	2	Pf2		1	1	2	none
	10	Fl1:4 Cl:2	4	2		6	Pf1 Pf2	3 1		2	6	Poss: 2LH instead MH
IV[1]	11	Fl1:1	1			1	Pf2	1			1	none
	12	Fl2:1 Tp:1 Pf:11	11→ 1	→ 1	→	13	Pf1 Pf2	11 1	1		13	none
	13	Fl1:1 Fl2:1 Tb:1	2		1	3	Pf2	2		1	3	none
	14	Fl1:1 Hn:1	1		1	2	Pf1 Pf2	 1	1		2	Poss: 1MH instead LH
	15	Fl3:2 Hn:3	2		3	5	Pf1 Pf2	2	 3		5	Poss: 3MH instead LH
	16	Fl3:7 Cl:4 Tp:2 Vc:3	7	6	3	16	Pf1 Pf2	4	3 2	 4	13	Missing: 3HH. Poss: 1LH instead MH
	17	Fl2:1 Fl3:6 Cl:3 Hn:1 Tb:4	7	3	5	15	Pf1 Pf2	 7		7	14	Missing: 1MH. Poss: 2LH instead MH
	18	Fl1:2 Fl3:3 Cl:2 Tb:1 Vc:2	5	2	3	10	Pf1 Pf2	5	2 3		10	Poss: 3LH instead MH
	19	Tb:2			2	2	Pf1			2	2	none
	20	Fl1:6 Tp:4 Vc:5 Db:3	6	4	8	18	Pf1 Pf2	6	5 7		18	Poss: 8MH instead LH

Rehearsal nr.	Ictus	Inst.	HH	MH	LH	Total	Inst.	HH	MH	LH	Total	Discrep.
V[1]	21	Fl2:5 Tp:9 Tb:1	5	9	1	15	Pf1			5	5	Missing: 5HH, 5LH. Poss: 4LH instead MH
	22	Fl1:3 Fl2:3 Fl3:3 Hn:7 Tb:8	9		15	24	Pf1 Pf2	6	1 9		16	Missing: 3HH, 5LH. Poss: 10MH instead LH
	23	Fl3:5 Cl:1 Tp:2	5	3		8	Pf1 Pf2		 5	1	6	Missing: 3MH. Poss: 5MH instead HH, 1LH instead MH
	24	Fl1:1 Tb:1	1		1	2	Pf1 Pf2	1		 1	2	none
	25	Fl3:10 Tb:9 Pf:16	16→ 10	→	→ 9	35	Pf1 Pf2		16 10		26	Missing: 9LH. Poss: 26MH instead HH
	26	Cl:2		2		2	Pf1			2	2	Poss: 2LH instead MH
	27	Cl:3 Tp:3		6		6	Pf1		5	1	6	Poss: 1LH instead MH
	28	Hn:2			2	2	Pf2			2	2	none
	29	Tb:1 Db:1			2	2	Pf1 Pf2		 1	1	2	Poss: 1MH instead LH
	30	Cl:2 Pf:3 Vc:5	3→	→ 2	→ 5	10	Pf1 Pf2	3	5	 2	10	Poss: 3MH instead LH
I[2]	31	Tb:1			1	1	Pf1			1	1	none
	32	Tb:3 Pf:1	1→	→	→ 3	4	Pf1 Pf2	2		 1	3	Missing: 1LH. Poss: 1 HH instead LH
	33	Cl:4 Tb:2 Db:2		4	4	8	Pf1 Pf2		 2	6	8	Poss: 2LH instead MH
	34	Fl3:1 Pf:9	9→ 1	→	→	10	Pf1 Pf2	5 5			10	none
	35	Cl:3 Hn:3		3	3	6	Pf1 Pf2		3	2 1	6	none
	36	Fl1:6 Fl2:5 Tp:5 Pf:17	17→ 11	→ 5	→	33	Pf1 Pf2	17	 11		28	Missing: 5MH. Poss: 11MH instead HH
	37	Fl1:4 Fl2:2 Fl3:4 Cl:4 Tp:3 Tb:3	10	7	3	20	Pf1 Pf2		6	2 5	13	Missing: 6 HH, 1MH. Poss: 4LH instead HH

Rehearsal nr.	Ictus	Inst.	HH	MH	LH	Total	Inst.	HH	MH	LH	Total	Discrep.
	38	Fl3:4 Cl:3 Hn:4 Tb:2 Vc:4	4	3	10	17	Pf1 Pf2		6	2 3	11	Missing: 1HH, 5LH. Poss: 4MH instead HH
	39	Fl1:6 Fl3:7 Cl:5 Hn:6 Tb:4 Vc:5	13	5	15	33	Pf1 Pf2		6 4	5	15	Missing: 10LH, 8HH. Poss: 5MH instead HH
	40	Fl1:2 Fl2:7 Db:3	9		3	12	Pf1 Pf2	4 5	2	1	12	Poss: 2MH instead LH

Discrepancies Page 3:

14 icti none
11 icti with fewer numbers in 2-piano version
0 icti with fewer numbers in ensemble version
0 icti empty in 2-piano version, but not in ensemble version
26 icti with numbers shifted in range.

Rehearsal nr.	Ictus	Inst.	HH	MH	LH	Total	Inst.	HH	MH	LH	Total	Discrep.
II[2]	1	Tp:5 Db:1		5	1	6	Pf1 Pf2		 5	1	6	none
	2	Fl1:1 Fl2:3 Tp:7 Vc:2	4	7	2	13	Pf1 Pf2	7 4	1 1		13	Poss: 7MH instead HH, 2 MH instead LH
	3	Fl2:2 Fl3:4	6			6	Pf1 Pf2	1 1	1 1	1 1	6	Poss: 2 MH instead HH, 2 LH instead HH
	4	Fl3:1 Hn:1	1		1	2	Pf1 Pf2	1	 1		2	Poss: 1MH instead LH
	5	Fl1:3 Tp:3 Db:2	3	3	2	8	Pf1 Pf2		5	 3	8	Poss: 2MH instead HH, 1 LH instead HH
	6	Fl1:2 Fl2:1 Fl3:4 Hn:3	7		3	10	Pf1 Pf2	2	1 3	4	10	Poss: 4MH instead HH, 1LH instead HH
	7	Cl:4 Tb:3		4	3	7	Pf1 Pf2			3 4	7	Poss: 4LH instead MH
	8	Cl:5 Tb:4 Db:3		5	7	12	Pf1 Pf2			5 2	7	Missing: 5MH
	9	Fl1:6 Fl3:3 Hn:4 Vc:4 Db:2	9		10	19	Pf1 Pf2	6 4	7 5		22	Extra: 1HH, 2 MH. Poss: 10 MH instead LH
	10	Fl3:5 Cl:7 Pf:11	11→ 5	→ 7	→	23	Pf1 Pf2	7 11	5	7	30	Extra: 5HH, 5LH. Poss: 2LH instead MH
III[2]	11	Tb:2 Pf:3	3→	→	→ 2	5	Pf1 Pf2		3	 2	5	Poss: 3MH instead HH
	12	Fl1:6 Pf:2	2→ 6	→	→	8	Pf1 Pf2	2 1		5	8	Poss: 5LH instead HH
	13	Fl1:1 Fl2:9 Fl3:6 Tp:5 Pf:8	8→ 16	→ 5	→	29	Pf1 Pf2	 4	8 5		17	Missing: 12HH
	14	Fl3:3 Cl:8	3	8		11	Empty				0	Missing: 3HH, 8MH
	15	Fl1:4 Cl:7 Pf:2	2→ 4	→ 7	→	13	Pf1 Pf2	2 4		7	13	Poss: 7LH instead MH
	16	Fl1:8 Cl:5 Db:3	8	5	3	16	Pf1 Pf2	8		 5	13	Missing: 3MH. Poss: 2LH instead MH
	17	Hn:4			4	4	Pf2		4		4	Poss: 4MH instead LH

Rehearsal nr.	Ictus	Inst.	HH	MH	LH	Total	Inst.	HH	MH	LH	Total	Discrep.
	18	Fl1:2 Cl:6 Hn:7 Vc:3	2	6	10	18	Pf1 Pf2	2	3	6 7	18	Poss: 3LH instead MH
	19	Fl1:4 Fl3:7 Tb:1 Pf:9 Vc:3	9→ 11	→	→ 4	24	Pf1 Pf2	9 3	 4	 1	17	Missing: 7HH. Poss: 4Mh instead LH, 1LH instead HH
	20	Fl1:1 Db:1	1		1	2	Pf1 Pf2	 1		1	2	none
IV²	21	Tp:4 Pf:1	1→	→ 4	→	5	Pf2		4	1	5	none
	22	Empty				0	Empty				0	none
	23	Fl2:6 Hn:3	6		3	9	Pf1 Pf2	4 2	 3		9	Poss: 3MH instead LH
	24	Fl2:1 Fl3:1	2			2	Pf1 Pf2	 1	1		2	Poss: 1MH instead HH
	25	Cl:3 Tb:5 Pf:12	12→	→ 3	→ 5	20	Pf1 Pf2	12	 4	 4	20	Poss: 1MH instead LH
	26	Vc:4			4	4	Pf1		4		4	Poss: 4MH instead LH
	27	Empty				0	Empty				0	none
	28	Vc:5 Db:3			8	8	Pf1 Pf2		 5	3	8	Poss: 5MH instead LH
	29	Fl1:6 Hn:5	6		5	11	Pf1 Pf2	 6	5		11	Poss: 5MH instead LH
	30	Fl2:1 Tb:3	1		3	4	Pf1 Pf2	1		 3	4	none
V²	31	Fl1:8 Fl3:5 Cl:7 Hn:4 Tp:6 Pf:11	11→ 13	→ 13	→ 4	41	Pf1 Pf2	6 4	5	 5	20	Missing: 13HH, 8MH.
	32	Fl3:1 Vc:2 Db:2	1		4	5	Pf1		1	2	3	Missing: 2LH. Poss: 1MH instead HH
	33	Fl2:4 Fl3:3	7			7	Pf1	4	3		7	Poss: 3MH instead HH
	34	Fl1:7 Fl3:6	13			13	Pf1 Pf2	2 6	2	3	13	Poss: 2MH instead HH, 3LH instead HH
	35	Fl2:8	8			8	Pf1 Pf2	6 2			8	none
	36	Fl1:1 Fl3:7	8			8	Pf1 Pf2		7 1		8	Poss: 8MH instead HH

Rehearsal nr.	Ictus	Inst.	HH	MH	LH	Total	Inst.	HH	MH	LH	Total	Discrep.
	37	Fl1:8 Fl2:6 Cl:5 Vc:4	14	5	4	23	Pf1 Pf2	8 6		5	19	Missing: 4MH. Poss: 1LH instead MH
	38	Fl1:1 Fl3:2 Tb:2 Pf:8	8→ 3	→	→ 2	13	Pf1 Pf2	8	3	 2	13	Poss: 3MH instead HH
	39	Empty				0	Empty				0	none
	40	Fl1:6 Fl2:7 Cl:2	13	2		15	Pf1 Pf2	6	7	 2	15	Poss: 7MH instead HH, 2LH instead MH

Discrepancies Page 4:

8 icti none
7 icti with fewer numbers in 2-piano version
2 icti with fewer numbers in ensemble version
1 ictus empty in 2-piano version, but not in ensemble version
28 icti with numbers shifted in range.

Rehearsal nr.	Ictus	Inst.	HH	MH	LH	Total	Inst.	HH	MH	LH	Total	Discrep.
I^3	1	Fl1:3 Fl2:4 Fl3:8 Pf:9	9→ 15	→	→	24	Pf1 Pf2	8 5	 4		17	Missing: 7HH
	2	Fl1: 8 Fl2:3 Tb:1	11		1	12	Pf1 Pf2		8 3	1	12	Poss: 11MH instead HH
	3	Fl1:4 Fl2:2 Fl3:5 Tp:6 Db:3	11	6	3	20	Pf1 Pf2	11	 6	 3	20	none
	4	Fl1:5 Fl2:3	8			8	Pf1 Pf2	 3	5		8	Poss: 5MH instead HH
	5	Fl1:2 Fl2:8 Fl3:1 Cl:5 Hn:4 Vc:5	11	5	9	25	Pf1 Pf2	11	3 5	2 5	26	Extra: 1MH, Poss: 2MH instead LH
	6	Fl1:5 Fl2:4 Fl3:3 Hn:2 Tp:6 Tb:1 Pf:7	7→ 12	→ 6	→ 3	28	Pf1 Pf2	7	3 2	 1	13	Missing: 12HH, 1MH, 2LH
	7	Fl3:6 Cl:7 Hn:3 Tb:5 Vc:4 Db:3	6	7	15	28	Pf1 Pf2		 3	7 5	15	Missing: 6HH, 4MH, 3LH
	8	Tp:7		7		7	Pf1 Pf2			7	7	Poss: 7LH instead MH
	9	Empty				0	Empty				0	none
	10	Fl1:6 Vc:5	6		5	11	Pf1	6	5		11	Poss: 5MH instead LH
II^3	11	Fl2:1 Tp:4	1	4		5	Pf1 Pf2	 1		4	5	Poss: 4LH instead MH
	12	Empty				0	Empty				0	none
	13	Cl:5 Pf:2	2→	→ 5	→	7	Pf1 Pf2	1 1		5	7	Poss: 5LH instead MH
	14	Vc:1			1	1	Pf1		1		1	Poss: 1MH instead LH
	15	Pf:4	4→	→	→	4	Pf1	4			4	none
	16	Empty				0	Empty				0	none
	17	Empty				0	Empty				0	none
	18	Empty				0	Empty				0	none

Rehearsal nr.	Ictus	Inst.	HH	MH	LH	Total	Inst.	HH	MH	LH	Total	Discrep.
	19	Pf:3	3→	→	→	3	Pf1	3			3	none
	20	Hn:1			1	1	Pf1		1		1	Poss: 1MH instead LH
III[3]	21	Empty				0	Empty				0	none
	22	Cl:4 Hn:3		4	3	7	Pf1 Pf2		3	4	7	Poss: 1LH instead MH
	23	Fl1:2 Fl2:5 Fl3:6 Db:2	13		2	15	Pf1 Pf2	2	5	5 3	15	Poss: 5MH instead HH, 6LH instead HH
	24	Vc:1			1	1	Pf2	1			1	Poss: 1HH instead LH
	25	Fl1:7 Fl3:7 Tp:6 Tb:5	14	6	5	25	Pf1 Pf2	14	6	5	25	none
	26	Hn:6 Tb:4 Pf:11 Vc:5 Db:4	11→	→	→ 19	30	Pf1 Pf2		11	7	18	Missing: 12LH
	27	Fl2:3 Fl3:5 Hn:4 Tb:2 Pf:4	4→ 8	→	→ 6	18	Pf1 Pf2	6		5 2	13	Missing: 4HH(?), 1LH
	28	Fl1:2 Fl2:6 Tp:4	8	4		12	Pf1 Pf2	6	6		12	Poss: 2MH instead HH
	29	Fl:4 Fl3:3 Cl:6 Tb:3 Db:1	7	6	4	17	Pf1 Pf2		4	9 1	14	Missing: 3HH, Poss: 4LH instead HH, 2LH instead MH
	30	Cl:5 Hn:5 Pf:2	2→	→ 5	→ 5	12	Pf1 Pf2	2	5	5	12	none
IV[3]	31	Fl3:7 Cl:3	7	3		10	Pf1 Pf2	7		3	10	Poss: 3LH instead MH
	32	Fl1:5 Fl2:6 Fl3:4 Cl:7 Tb:6	15	7	6	28	Pf1 Pf2	11		7	18	Missing: 4HH, 6MH, Poss: 1LH instead MH
	33	Fl1:3 Fl2:4 Fl3:5 Hn:4	12		4	16	Pf1 Pf2	6	6 4		16	Poss: 6MH instead HH, 4MH instead LH

Rehearsal nr.	Ictus	Inst.	HH	MH	LH	Total	Inst.	HH	MH	LH	Total	Discrep.
	34	Fl2:6 Cl:2 Tp:5 Tb:1 Db:2	6	7	3	16	Pf1 Pf2		6	5 5	16	Poss: 6LH instead HH, 1LH instead MH
	35	Fl2:1 Cl:1 Hn:1	1	1	1	3	Pf1 Pf2	1	 1	1	3	none
	36	Fl1:3 Pf:3	3→ 3	→	→	6	Pf1 Pf2	 1	5		6	none
	37	Fl3:5 Hn:3 Tb:1 Vc:1	5		5	10	Pf1 Pf2	5	3 1	 1	10	Poss: 4MH instead LH
	38	Empty				0	Empty				0	none
	39	Tp:1 Vc:4 Db:1		1	5	6	Pf1 Pf2	 1	4	 1	6	Poss: 1HH instead LH, 3MH instead LH
	40	Fl1:2 Cl:5 Hn:2 Pf:7	7→ 2	→ 5	→ 2	16	Pf1 Pf2	9	 2	 5	16	Poss: 3LH instead MH

Discrepancies Page 5:

14 icti none
7 icti with fewer numbers in 2-piano version
1 ictus with fewer numbers in ensemble version
0 icti empty in 2-piano version, but not in ensemble version
21 icti with numbers shifted in range.

Rehearsal nr.	Ictus	Inst.	HH	MH	LH	Total	Inst.	HH	MH	LH	Total	Discrep.
V³	1	Fl2:7 Fl3:5 Tp:3 Pf:8 Vc:4	8→ 12	→ 3	→ 4	27	Pf1 Pf2	8		 4	12	Missing: 12HH, 3MH
	2	Fl1:6 Cl:5 Hn:3	6	5	3	14	Pf1 Pf2		9 5		14	Poss: 6MH instead HH, 3MH instead LH
	3	Hn:1 Pf:4	4→	→	→ 1	5	Pf1 Pf2	 4		1	5	none
	4	Tb:2			2	2	Pf2			2	2	none
	5	Tp:5 Db:4		5	4	9	Pf1 Pf2		5 4		9	Poss: 4MH instead LH
	6	Hn:1			1	1	Pf2			1	1	none
	7	Fl1:7 Fl2:5 Fl3:6 Hn:5 Tp:7 Tb:3 Pf:9 Db:5	9→ 18	→ 7	→ 13	47	Pf1 Pf2	9 7			16	Missing: 11HH, 7MH, 13LH
	8	Fl1:9 Fl2:6 Fl3:4 Cl:7 Hn:2 Tp:5 Vc:7	19	12	9	40	Pf1 Pf2		10	 7	17	Missing: 19HH, 2MH, 2LH
	9	Fl1:5 Fl2:4 Fl3:7 Cl:5 Hn:4 Tp:3 Tb:4 Db:2	16	8	10	34	Pf1 Pf2		 7	9	16	Missing:16HH, 1MH, 1LH
	10	Fl1:6 Fl2:7 Fl3:5 Cl:6 Hn:1 Tp:6 Tb:6 Db:6	18	12	13	43	Pf1 Pf2	6 5	7 2	5	24	Missing: 7HH, 3MH, 8LH

Rehearsal nr.	Ictus	Inst.	HH	MH	LH	Total	Inst.	HH	MH	LH	Total	Discrep.
I^4	11	Fl1:3 Fl3:3 Tp:5	6	5		11	Pf1 Pf2	3	3	5 4	15	Extra:4LH, poss: 3LH instead HH, 2LH instead MH
	12	Fl1:5 Hn:5 Tp:9 Tb:2	5	9	7	21	Pf1 Pf2	 5	9 5	2	21	Poss: 5MH instead LH
	13	Fl2:6 Cl:7	6	7		13	Pf1 Pf2	6		 7	13	Poss: 7LH instead MH
	14	Tp:3		3		3	Pf1		3		3	none
	15	Cl:2 Hn:4 Tp:5		7	4	11	Pf1 Pf2	7 1	 5	4 2	19	Extra: 6 HH, 2LH, poss: 2HH instead MH
	16	Tb:3			3	3	Pf1 Pf2			2 1	3	none
	17	Cl:2 Hn:1		2	1	3	Pf1 Pf2		1	 2	3	Poss: 1LH instead MH
	18	Fl3:5 Cl:6 Vc:3	5	6	3	14	Pf1 Pf2	1 5	2	6	14	Poss: 1LH instead HH, 4LH instead MH
	19	Empty				0	Empty				0	none
	20	Tb:2			2	2	Pf1			2	2	none
II^4	21	Fl1:7 Fl2:3 Cl:6 Hn:4 Pf:6	6→ 10	→ 6	→ 4	26	Pf1 Pf2	6		 6	12	Missing:10HH, 4MH, Poss: 2LH instead MH
	22	Fl1:9 Fl3:5 Tp:2 Pf:9	9→ 14	→ 2	→	25	Pf1 Pf2		9 2		11	Missing:14HH
	23	Fl2:6 Tp:4 Tb:3	6	4	3	13	Pf1 Pf2	6	 4	 3	13	none
	24	Hn:2 Pf:3	3→	→	→ 2	5	Pf1 Pf2	3 1	 1		5	Poss: 1HH instead LH, 1MH instead MH
	25	Hn:5			5	5	Pf1		5		5	Poss: 5MH instead LH
	26	Pf:4	4→	→	→	4	Pf1	4			4	none
	27	Hn:1 Pf:7	7→	→	→ 1	8	Pf1 Pf2	7	 1		8	Poss: 1MH instead LH
	28	Hn:3 Pf:16	16→	→	→ 3	19	Pf1 Pf2	6	5 3	5	19	none

Rehearsal nr.	Ictus	Inst.	HH	MH	LH	Total	Inst.	HH	MH	LH	Total	Discrep.
	29	Fl1:11 Hn:3 Tp:8 Pf:2	2→ 11	→ 8	→ 3	24	Pf1 Pf2	11 4	 4		19	Missing: 2MH, 3LH
	30	Hn:6			6	6	Pf2		6		6	Poss: 6MH instead LH
III[4]	31	Pf:11	11→	→	→	11	Pf1	11			11	none
	32	Empty				0	Empty				0	none
	33	Empty				0	Empty				0	none
	34	Fl2:9 Fl3:14 Hn:5 Tp:7 Tb:9 Pf:5 Vc:6 Db:7	5→ 23	→ 7	→ 27	62	Pf1 Pf2	7	7	 9	23	Missing: 21HH, 18LH
	35	Fl1:2 Fl2:2 Cl:2 Hn:5	4	2	5	11	Pf1 Pf2	 4	5	2	11	Poss: 3MH instead LH
	36	Empty				0	Empty				0	none
	37	Vc:1			1	1	Pf1			1	1	none
	38	Fl2:2 Tp:9 Db:1	2	9	1	12	Pf1 Pf2	9 2		 1	12	Poss: 9HH instead MH
	39	Fl1:7 Fl2:6 Fl3:9 Cl:7	22	7		29	Pf1 Pf2		6 5	7 4	22	Missing: 7HH, Poss:4MH instead HH, 11LH instead HH
	40	Fl1:4 Fl2:6 Tp:8 Pf:10	10→ 10	→ 8	→	28	Pf1 Pf2	10 4	 4		18	Missing: 6HH, 4MH

Discrepancies Page 6:

15 icti none
11 icti with fewer numbers in 2-piano version
2 icti with fewer numbers in ensemble version
0 icti empty in 2-piano version, but not in ensemble version
16 icti with numbers shifted in range.

Rehearsal nr.	Ictus	Inst.	HH	MH	LH	Total	Inst.	HH	MH	LH	Total	Discrep.
IV4	1	Cl:4 Tp: 5 Pf:9	9→	→ 9	→	18	Pf1 Pf2		9 5	 4	18	Poss: 4LH instead MH
	2	Fl1:1	1			1	Pf1	1			1	none
	3	Empty				0	Empty				0	none
	4	Pf:8	8→	→	→	8	Pf1			8	8	none
	5	Empty				0	Empty				0	none
	6	Empty				0	Empty				0	none
	7	Pf:3	3→	→	→	3	Pf1	3			3	none
	8	Empty				0	Empty				0	none
	9	Hn:2 Tb:2			4	4	Pf1 Pf2		2	1 1	4	Poss: 2MH instead LH
	10	Tp:4 Tb:1		4	1	5	Pf1 Pf2	1	3 1		5	Poss: 1HH instead LH
V4	11	Fl1:2 Cl:7 Hn:1 Db:4	2	7	5	14	Pf1 Pf2	 2		7	9	Missing: MH, Poss: 2lh instead MH
	12	Empty				0	Empty				0	none
	13	Fl1:2	2			2	Pf1 Pf2	1 1			2	none
	14	Fl2:5 Fl3:7 Cl:3 Tp:6 Tb:2	12	9	2	23	Pf1 Pf2	5	7	 5	17	Missing: 6HH, Poss: 1LH instead HH, 2LH instead MH
	15	Hn:1 Pf:13	13→	→	→ 1	14	Pf1 Pf2	1	6 1	6	14	Poss: 1MH instead LH
	16	Fl1:7 Fl2:4 Tp:5 Tb:5 Pf:5 Vc:4	5→ 13	→ 5	→ 9	32	Pf1 Pf2	5	5	6 5	21	Missing:11HH, Poss: 2lH instead HH
	17	Hn:2 Tb:1			3	3	Pf2			1	1	Missing: 2LH
	18	Fl2:9 Tp:7 Tb:5 Pf:2 Db:4	2→ 9	→ 7	→ 9	27	Pf1 Pf2		9	 5	14	Missing:11HH, 2LH, Poss: 2 MH instead LH
	19	Fl3:9 Hn:4 Tp:3 Vc:9	9	3	13	25	Pf1 Pf2	9 3	 4		16	Missing:3HH, 6LH Poss: 1MH instead LH
	20	Fl2:5 Cl:6 Hn:8 Tb:7 Db:2	5	6	17	28	Pf1 Pf2		 5	13 2	20	Missing:5HH, 1MH, 2LH

Rehearsal nr.	Ictus	Inst.	HH	MH	LH	Total	Inst.	HH	MH	LH	Total	Discrep.
I[5]	21	Fl1:5 Fl3:1 Cl:3 Tp:9 Tb:2 Vc:2	6	12	4	22	Pf1 Pf2		5	4 3	12	Missing: 6HH, 4MH, Poss: 3LH instead MH
	22	Cl:3 Tp:1 Tb:2 Vc:1 Db:3		4	6	10	Pf1 Pf2	1		 5	6	Missing: 3MH, 1LH, Poss: 1HH instead MH
	23	Fl1:2	2			2	Pf1		1	1	2	Poss: 1MH instead HH, 1LH instead HH
	24	Hn:2 Tb:4			6	6	Pf1 Pf2	1	1 1	1 1	5	Missing: 1LH, Poss: 1HH instead LH, 2MH instead LH
	25	Tp:4 Db:2		4	2	6	Pf1 Pf2	1 1	1 1	1 1	6	Poss: 2HH instead MH
	26	Fl1:4 Cl:2 Tb:4 Pf:11 Vc:5	11→ 4	→ 2	→ 9	26	Pf1 Pf2:	6	5	 6	17	Missing: 4HH, 2MH, 3LH
	27	Fl2:2	2			2	Pf1	1		1	2	Poss: 1LH instead HH
	28	Fl1:5	5			5	Pf1	5			5	none
	29	Pf:7	7→	→	→	7	Pf1		7		7	none
	30	Fl1:2 Pf:9	9→ 2	→	→	11	Pf1 Pf2	6 5			11	none
II[5]	31	Hn:5			5	5	Pf1		5		5	Poss: 5MH instead LH
	32	Tp:1 Pf:3	3→	→ 1	→	4	PF1	3	1		4	none
	33	Tb:2			2	2	Pf1 Pf2			1 1	2	none
	34	Hn:1			1	1	Pf1		1		1	Poss: 1MH instead LH
	35	Fl1:6 Cl:4 Hn:5	6	4	5	15	Pf1 Pf2		5	6 4	15	Poss: 6LH instead HH, 1MH instead LH

Rehearsal nr.	Ictus	Inst.	HH	MH	LH	Total	Inst.	HH	MH	LH	Total	Discrep.
	36	Fl1:2 Fl2:4 Tp:3 Tb:1 Pf:7 Db:2	7→ 6	→ 3	→ 3	19	Pf1 Pf2	9	 7		16	Missing:3HH, Poss: 1MH instead HH, 3MH Instead LH
	37	Fl2:7 Fl3:5 Tp:2 Tb:3	12	2	3	17	Pf1 Pf2	 5		6	11	Missing: 6HH, Poss: 1LH instead HH, 2LH instead MH
	38	Fl3:4 Tp:6 Vc:3	4	6	3	13	Pf1 Pf2		7	 6	13	Poss: 1MH instead HH, 3LH instead HH
	39	Fl1:7 Fl2:6 Fl3:3 Cl:7 Tb:2	16	7	2	25	Pf1 Pf2		 7	9	16	Missing: 9HH, Poss: 7LH instead HH
	40	Fl2:5 Cl:3 Hn:4 Tb:6 Pf:13	13→ 5	→ 3	→ 10	31	Pf1 Pf2	7 5	6		18	Missing: 13LH

Discrepancies Page 7:

14 icti none
15 icti with fewer numbers in 2-piano version
0 icti with fewer numbers in ensemble version
0 icti empty in 2-piano version, but not in ensemble version
22 icti with numbers shifted in range.

Rehearsal nr.	Ictus	Inst.	HH	MH	LH	Total	Inst.	HH	MH	LH	Total	Discrep.
III[5]	1	Fl1:9 Fl2:5 Fl3:8 Tb:4	22		4	26	Pf1 Pf2		9	 4	13	Missing: 13HH, Poss: 9MH instead HH
	2	Fl3:6 Cl:5 Hn:3 Tp:1 Pf:13	13→ 6	→ 6	→ 3	28	Pf1 Pf2	13		 5	18	Missing: 6HH, 4MH, Poss: 2LH instead MH
	3	Fl1:8 Fl2:5 Fl3:8 Tp:6 Pf:9 Db:4	9→ 21	→ 6	→ 4	40	Pf1 Pf2	9	 4		13	Missing: 21HH, 2MH, 4LH
	4	Fl1:2 Hn:1 Vc:5	2		6	8	Pf1 Pf2		7 1		8	Poss: 2MH instead HH, 6MH instead LH
	5	Fl3:8 Tp:2 Pf:2 Vc:7 Db:6	2→ 8	→ 2	→ 13	25	Pf1 Pf2	2 8	7	6	23	Missing: 2LH, Poss: 5MH instead LH
	6	Fl1:8 Fl2:9 Cl:2 Hn:3 Tp:5 Tb:6 Vc:7 Db:5	17	7	21	45	Pf2		6	7	13	Missing: 17HH, 1MH, 14LH
	7	Fl1:4 Fl2:2 Fl3:3 Cl:7 Hn:4 Tb:7 Pf:14	14→ 9	→ 7	→ 11	41	Pf1	14			14	Missing: 9HH, 7MH, 11LH
	8	Fl2:4 Tp:3 Tb:2 Pf:6	6→ 4	→ 3	→ 2	15	Pf1 Pf2	6	7	 2	15	Poss: 4MH instead HH
	9	Empty				0	Empty				0	none
	10	Hn:1 Pf:5	5→	→	→ 1	6	Pf1 Pf2	5	 1		6	Poss: 1MH instead LH
IV[5]	11	Hn:4			4	4	Pf2			4	4	none
	12	Pf:9	9→	→	→	9	Pf1	9			9	none
	13	Empty				0	Empty				0	none

Rehearsal nr.	Ictus	Inst.	HH	MH	LH	Total	Inst.	HH	MH	LH	Total	Discrep.
	14	Empty				0	Empty				0	none
	15	Hn:1			1	1	Pf1		1		1	Poss: 1MH insteadLH
	16	Empty				0	Empty				0	none
	17	Empty				0	Empty				0	none
	18	Hn:3 Vc:5			8	8	Pf1 Pf2		5 3		8	Poss: 8MH instead LH
	19	Cl:2 Tp:4 Tb:1 Pf:7	7→	→ 6	→ 1	14	Pf1 Pf2	7	 4	 3	14	Poss: 2LH instead MH
	20	Hn:1 Tb:2 Db:3			6	6	Pf1 Pf2		 1	5	6	Poss: 1MH instead LH
V[5]	21	Fl1:6 Cl:4 Hn:3	6	4	3	13	Pf1 Pf2	6	 3	4	13	Poss: 1LH instead MH
	22	Empty				0	Empty				0	none
	23	Cl:2 Vc:3 Db:2		2	5	7	Pf1 Pf2		3	2 2	7	Poss: 1MH instead LH
	24	Cl:7 Tp:3		10		10	Pf1 Pf2		3	 7	10	Poss: 7LH instead MH
	25	Cl:4 Tp:5		9		9	Pf1 Pf2	5		 4	9	Poss: 5HH instead MH, 4LH instead MH
	26	Hn:6 Tp:4 Tb:3 Db:5		4	14	18	Pf1 Pf2	4	6	3 5	18	Poss: 4HH instead LH, 2MH instead LH,
	27	Fl1:2 Fl3:7 Cl:5 Hn:1 Tb:4	9	5	5	19	Pf1 Pf2	7	 5	 4	16	Missing: 2HH, 1LH
	28	Fl2:4 Cl:6 Tp:1 Vc:6	4	7	6	17	Pf1 Pf2	 4	 1	6	11	Missing: 6MH
	29	Fl1:8 Fl2:3 Fl3:6 Tp:2 Tb:3	17	2	3	22	Pf1 Pf2		8	 3	11	Missing: 11HH, Poss: 6MH instead HH
	30	Hn:2 Tp:6 Tb:1		6	3	9	Pf1 Pf2	 2	6 1		9	Poss: 2HH, instead LH

Rehearsal nr.	Ictus	Inst.	HH	MH	LH	Total	Inst.	HH	MH	LH	Total	Discrep.
16	31	Hn:4			4		Pf1 Pf2		1 1	1 1	4	Poss: 2MH instead LH
	32	Tp:3 Tb:5 Db:4		3	9	12	Pf1 Pf2		3 4	5	12	Poss: 4MH instead LH
	33	Cl:7 Hn:6 Tp:4 Tb:4 Vc:3		11	13	24	Pf1 Pf2	 6	 4	11	21	Missing: 1MH, 2LH, Poss: 6HH instead MH
	34	Cl:4 Hn:3 Vc:4 Db:2		4	9	13	Pf1 Pf2		3	2 4	9	Missing: 1MH, 6LH
	35	Fl1:5 Fl3:7 Cl:5 Tp:3 Tb:4 Pf:3	3→ 12	→ 8	→ 4	27	Pf1 Pf2	8	 5	 4	17	Missing: 4(7) HH, 3(6)MH
	36	Fl1:2 Fl2:6 Fl3:4 Hn:5 Tp:8 Tb:1 Vc:6	12	8	12	32	Pf1 Pf2	 7	8		15	Missing: 5HH, 12LH
	37	Fl1:1 Tp:2 Db:1	1	2	1	4	Pf1 Pf2	1	 2	 1	4	none
	38	Fl2:2 Hn:4 Tp:2 Tb:3	2	2	7	11	Pf1 Pf2	2 2	4	3	11	Poss: 2HH instead LH, 2MH instead LH
	39	Hn:1			1	1	Pf1		1		1	Poss: 1MH instead LH
	40	Empty				0	Empty				0	none

Discrepancies Page 8:

10 icti none
13 icti with fewer numbers in 2-piano version
0 icti with fewer numbers in ensemble version
0 icti empty in 2-piano version, but not in ensemble version
22 icti with numbers shifted in range.

Rehearsal nr.	Ictus	Inst.	HH	MH	LH	Total	Inst.	HH	MH	LH	Total	Discrep.
II^{6}	1	Fl1:3 Hn:2 Pf:9	9→ 3	→	→ 2	14	Pf1 Pf2	7 7			14	Poss: 2HH instead LH
	2	Fl3:6 Cl:5 Tp:4 Vc:3	6	9	3	18	Pf1 Pf2		7 5	3	15	Missing: 3HH, Poss: 3MH instead HH
	3	Cl:3 Hn:7 Tp:2 Db:1		5	8	13	Pf1 Pf2	 2	7	 4	13	Poss: 2HH instead LH, 2MH instead LH
	4	Pf:16	16→	→	→	16	Pf1	16			16	none
	5	Empty				0	Empty				0	none
	6	Pf:5	5→	→	→	5	Pf1	5			5	none
	7	Fl2:5 Hn:4 Tb:6	5		10	15	Pf1 Pf2	4	5	 6	15	Poss: 1MH instead HH, 4MH instead LH
	8	Fl1:7 Fl3:8	15			15	Pf1 Pf2	 7	8		15	Poss: 8MH instead HH
	9	Vc:5			5	5	Pf2		5		5	Poss: 5MH instead LH
	10	Fl1:4 Fl2:8 Fl3:3 Tp:6 Tb:4 Pf:7	7→ 15	→ 6	→ 4	32	Pf1 Pf2	11 6			17	Missing: 11MH(?), 4LH
III^{6}	11	Fl1:3 Fl3:7 Tb:5	10		5	15	Pf1 Pf2		10	 5	15	Poss: 10MH instead HH
	12	Fl2:5 Cl:9 Hn:3	5	9	3	17	Pf1 Pf2		 3	9	12	Missing: 5HH, Poss: 6LH instead MH
	13	Fl1:8 Cl:7 Hn:4 Db:5	8	7	9	24	Pf1 Pf2		8	 7	15	Missing: 8HH, 1LH, Poss: 1MH instead LH
	14	Fl2:6 Cl:4 Hn:2 Pf:9 Vc:7	9→ 6	→ 4	→ 9	28	Pf1 Pf2	6	7	 4	17	Missing: 9LH(?)
	15	Fl1:4 Fl2:6 Fl3:3 Tp:7 Tb:1 Vc:4 Db:2	13	7	7	27	Pf1 Pf2	13 1	 4	 3	21	Missing: 2MH, 4LH, Poss: 1HH instead LH, 2MH instead LH

Rehearsal nr.	Ictus	Inst.	HH	MH	LH	Total	Inst.	HH	MH	LH	Total	Discrep.
	16	Fl1:5 Cl:4 Pf:8 Db:4	8→ 5	→ 4	→ 4	21	Pf1 Pf2		8 4		12	Missing: 5HH, 4LH
	17	Fl1:7 Fl2:8 Fl3:9 Tp:6 Tb:2 Db:1	24	6	3	33	Pf2			3	3	Missing: 24HH, 6MH
	18	Fl2:3 Cl:12 Hn:4 Pf:18	18→ 3	→ 12	→ 4	37	Pf1 Pf2	18	 5	 5	28	Missing: 3HH, 7MH, 4LH
	19	Hn:3 Vc:5 Db:2			10	10	Pf2	5		5	10	Poss: 5HH instead LH
	20	Fl2:11 Fl3:4 Cl:1 Tb:2 Vc:3	15	1	5	21	Pf1 Pf2	11 1	 1	 2	15	Missing:3HH, 3LH
IV[6]	21	Fl2:4 Fl3:1 Cl:5 Tp:4 Tb:1 Vc:5	6	9	6	21	Pf1 Pf2		9	1 6	16	Missing: 5HH, Poss: 1LH instead HH
	22	Fl3:6 Hn:4 Tp:10 Tb:2 Pf:1 Vc:2	1→ 6	→ 10	→ 8	25	Pf1 Pf2	7	 4	 2	13	Missing: 6MH, 6LH
	23	Fl1:5 Fl2:4	9			9	Pf1 Pf2	 4	5		9	Poss: 5MH instead HH
	24	Fl1:1 Tp:5 Tb:5 Vc:4 Db:2	1	5	11	17	Pf1 Pf2	5	4	 5	14	Missing: 3LH, Poss: 4HH instead LH, 1MH instead LH
	25	Fl1:9 Fl2:7 Cl:3 Pf:3 Vc:2	3→ 16	→ 3	→ 2	24	Pf1 Pf2	1	9	 3	13	Missing: 11HH, Poss:3M instead HH, 1LH instead HH
	26	Tp:6 Tb:1		6	1	7	Pf1 Pf2		6	 1	7	none

Rehearsal nr.	Ictus	Inst.	HH	MH	LH	Total	Inst.	HH	MH	LH	Total	Discrep.
	27	Cl:7		7		7	Pf1			7	7	Poss: 7LH instead MH
	28	Fl1:8 Tp:1 Tb:3	8	1	3	12	Pf1 Pf2	6 3		 3	12	Poss: 1HH instead MH
	29	Fl1:2 Fl2:1 Hn:4 Tp:3	3	3	4	10	Pf1 Pf2		5 5		10	Poss: 3MH instead HH, 4MH instead LH
	30	Empty				0	Empty				0	none
V^{6}	31	Fl1:7 Cl:1 Hn:2 Tb:6	7	1	8	16	Pf1 Pf2	7		1 6	14	Missing: 1MH, 1LH
	32	Fl1:2 Vc:5	2		5	7	Pf1		2		2	Missing: 5LH, Poss: 2MH instead HH
	33	Fl1:1 Pf:4	4→ 1	→	→	5	Pf1	1			1	Missing: 4HH(?)
	34	Fl1:8 Pf:17	17→ 8	→	→	25	Pf1	8			8	Missing: 17HH(?)
	35	Fl1:3 Hn:4 Tp:7 Db:2	3	7	6	16	Pf1 Pf2	3	4 7	2	16	Poss: 4MH instead LH
	36	Pf:5	5→	→	→	5	Pf1		5		5	none
			HL	ML	LL			HL	ML	LL		
	37	Fl3:7 Cl:4 Hn:3 Tp:5 Tb:4 Pf:11 Vc:9 Db:7	11→ 16	→ 16	→ 7	50	Pf1 Pf2	11		7 8	24	Missing: 16HL, 8ML, Poss: 8LL instead ML
	38	Fl1:6 Fl2:5 Fl3:3 Cl:7 Tp:1 Tb:2 Pf:4	4→ 22	→ 2	→	28	Pf1 Pf2	6	5 9	7	27	Missing: 1HH, Poss: 12ML instead HL, 7LL instead HL

Rehearsal nr.	Ictus	Inst.	HH	MH	LH	Total	Inst.	HH	MH	LH	Total	Discrep.
	39	Fl1:3 Fl2:4 Fl3:1 Cl:3 Hn:5 Tp:6 Pf:7 Vc:4 Db:2	7→ 17	→ 9	→ 2	35	Pf1 Pf2	 5	11		16	Missing: 12HL, 7LL
	40	Cl:1 Hn:4 Tb:3	1	7		8	Pf1 Pf2	4		 4	8	Poss: 3HL instead ML, 4LL instead ML

Discrepancies Page 9:

6 icti none
21 icti with fewer numbers in 2-piano version
0 icti with fewer numbers in ensemble version
0 icti empty in 2-piano version, but not in ensemble version
23 icti with numbers shifted in range.

Rehearsal nr.	Ictus	Inst.	HL	ML	LL	Total	Inst.	HL	ML	LL	Total	Discrep.
I^{7}	1	Fl1:8 Hn:1 Tp:3	11	1		12	Pf1 Pf2		8 4		12	Poss: 10ML instead HL
	2	Fl1:4 Fl2:3 Tp:5 Pf:2	2→ 12	→	→	14	Pf1 Pf2	9		 5	14	Poss:3LL instead HL
	3	Fl1:7 Fl2:2 Fl3:8 Cl:5 Tb:4	22	4		26	Pf1 Pf2	7	2	5 4	18	Missing: 8HL, Poss: 7LL instead HL, 2LL instead ML
	4	Fl3:3 Cl:1 Vc:6	4	6		10	Pf1 Pf2	3	6	 1	10	Poss: 1LL instead HL
	5	Fl3:6 Hn:3 Db:1	6		4	10	Pf1 Pf2	6	3	 1	10	Poss: 3ML instead LL
	6	Cl:2 Pf:8 Vc:4	8→ 2	→ 4	→	14	Pf1 Pf2	8 4		2	14	Poss: 2HL instead ML, 2LL instead ML
	7	Fl1:4 Tp:8 Tb:6 Db:5	4	8	11	23	Pf1 Pf2		8	 6	14	Missing: 4HL, 5LL
	8	Fl1:3 Fl2:1 Cl:1 Hn:4 Tp:3 Tb:2 Db:4	8	6	4	18	Pf1 Pf2	7	 3	5	15	Missing: 1HL, 2ML, Poss: 1LL instead ML
	9	Fl1:6 Fl2:5 Fl3:2 Cl:4 Vc:3	17	3		20	Pf1 Pf2		11	 4	15	Missing: 5HL, Poss: 8ML instead HL, 4LL instead HL
	10	Fl2:7 Fl3:1 Cl:3 Tp:5 Vc:5 Db:3	16	5	3	24	Pf1 Pf2			8 6	14	Missing: 10HL, Poss: 6LL instead HL, 5LL instead ML
II^{7}	11	Fl3:4 Cl:9 Hn:3 Tp:4 Tb:1	17	4		21	Pf1 Pf2		 7	9	16	Missing: 5HL, Poss: 3ML instead HL, 9LL instead HL

Rehearsal nr.	Ictus	Inst.	HL	ML	LL	Total	Inst.	HL	ML	LL	Total	Discrep.
	12	Fl1:1 Cl:5 Hn:1 Tp:6 Tb:3	12	4		16	Pf1 Pf2	1 7	8		16	Poss: 4ML instead HL
	13	Fl1:3 Hn:2 Vc:2	3	4		7	Pf1 Pf2	3	2	 2	7	Poss: 2LL instead ML
	14	Fl1:2 Cl:1 Db:1	3		1	4	Pf1 Pf2	1 1	1	1	4	Poss: 1ML instead HL
	15	Fl1:7 Fl3:4 Cl:3 Tb:2	14	2		16	Pf1 Pf2	6	5	 5	16	Poss: 3ML instead HL, 5LL instead HL
	16	Fl3:2 Cl:6 Hn:1	8	1		9	Pf1 Pf2		2	 6	8	Missing: 1HL, Poss: 1ML instead HL, 6LL instead HL
	17	Fl3:9 Cl:4	13			13	Pf1 Pf2			9 4	13	Poss: 13LL instead HL
	18	Fl3:5 Cl:2	7			7	Pf1 Pf2			5 2	7	Poss: 7LL instead HL
	19	Fl3:4 Cl:1	5			5	Pf1 Pf2			4 1	5	Poss: 5LL instead HL
	20	Fl3:6 Cl:7	13			13	Pf1 Pf2			6 7	13	Poss: 13LL instead HL
III[7]	21	Fl3:2 Cl:3	5			5	Pf1 Pf2			2 3	5	Poss: 5LL instead HL
	21A						Extra ictus only in 2PF version				0	Extra
			HH	MH	LH			HH	MH	LH		
	22	Fl1:9 Fl2:8 Tp:7	17	7		24	Pf1 Pf2	9 7	8		24	Poss: 1MH instead HH
	23	Empty				0	Empty				0	none
	24	Vc:2			2	2	Pf1		2		2	Poss: 2MH instead LH
	25	Empty				0	Empty				0	none
	26	Empty				0	Empty				0	none
	27	Fl1:5 Hn:1 Pf:13	13→ 5	→ 1	→	19	Pf1 Pf2	11	 7		18	Missing: 1HH, Poss: 6MH instead HH?
	28	Empty				0	Empty				0	none
	29	Empty				0	Empty				0	none
	30	Empty				0	Empty				0	none

Rehearsal nr.	Ictus	Inst.	HL	ML	LL	Total	Inst.	HL	ML	LL	Total	Discrep.
IV⁷	31	Hn:2 Tp:1 Vc:1		1	3	4	Pf1 Pf2	1	1	1 1	4	Poss: 1HH instead LH
	32	Empty				0	Empty				0	none
	33	Empty				0	Empty				0	none
	34	Empty				0	Empty				0	none
	35	Empty				0	Empty				0	none
	36	Hn:3		3		3	Pf1		3		3	none
	37	Empty				0	Empty				0	none
	38	Cl:1		1		1	Pf1			1	1	Poss: 1LH instead MH
	39	Fl2:2 Cl:4 Pf:7	7→ 2	→ 4	→	13	Pf1 Pf2	5 1	1 2	4	12	Missing: 1HH, Poss: 1LH instead MH?
	40	Fl1:4 Tp:1 Tb:1 Pf:2 Vc:3	2→ 4	→ 1	→ 4	11	Pf1 Pf2	7	3	1	11	Poss: 1 HH instead LH, 2MH instead LH

Discrepancies Page 10:

12 icti none
9 icti with fewer numbers in 2-piano version
0 icti with fewer numbers in ensemble version
1 ictus empty in 2-piano version, but not in ensemble version, but this is an extra ictus, occurring only in the 2-piano version
27 icti with numbers shifted in range.

Rehearsal nr.	Ictus	Inst.	HH	MH	LH	Total	Inst.	HH	MH	LH	Total	Discrep.
V^7	1	Fl3:5 Hn:4 Tp:2 Pf:9	9→ 5	→ 2	→ 4	20	Pf1 Pf2	 6	9	5	20	Poss: 1HH instead MH, 1 LH instead MH
	2	Fl1:1	1			1	Pf1	1			1	none
	3	Empty				0	Empty				0	none
	4	Cl:2 Tp:1 Db:1		3	1	4	Pf1 Pf2		 1	3	4	Poss: 2LH instead MH
	5	Pf:5	5→	→	→	5	Pf1	5			5	none
	6	Pf:11 Vc:5	11→	→	→ 5	16	Pf1	6	5		11	Missing: 5LH
	7	Pf:4	4→	→	→	4	Pf1 Pf2	1 3			4	none
	8	Pf:1	1→	→	→	1	Pf2		1			none
	9	Hn:4 Pf:7	7→	→	→ 4	11	Pf1		11		11	Poss: 4MH instead LH
	10	Cl:5		5		5	Pf1			5	5	Poss: 5LH instead MH
I^8	11	Pf:4	4→	→	→	4	Pf1	3	1		4	none
	12	Empty				0	Empty				0	none
	13	Empty				0	Empty				0	none
	14	Empty				0	Empty				0	none
	15	Vc:1			1	1	Pf2		1		1	Poss: 1MH instead LH
	16	Empty				0	Empty				0	none
	17	Empty				0	Empty				0	none
	18	Fl1:7 Fl2:6 Fl3:4 Hn:3 Tp:6 Pf:18 Db:3	18→ 17	→ 6	→ 6	47	Pf1 Pf2	9	 11	9	29	Missing: 12HH, 6LH, Poss: 5MH instead HH
	19	Fl1:5 Fl3:9 Cl:2 Hn:1 Vc:6	14	2	7	23	Pf1 Pf2	 5	11		16	Missing: 7LH, Poss: 9MH instead HH
	20	Fl2:4 Fl3:6 Cl:1 Hn:4 Tp:6 Vc:8 Db:7	10	7	19	36	Pf1 Pf2			10 7	17	Missing: 10HH, 7MH, 2LH

Rehearsal nr.	Ictus	Inst.	HH	MH	LH	Total	Inst.	HH	MH	LH	Total	Discrep.
II[8]	21	Fl1:3 Fl2:7 Fl3:2 Tp:6 Tb:4 Vc:3 Db:4	12	6	13	31	Pf1 Pf2		12 9		21	Missing: 10LH(?),Poss: 12MH instead HH, 3MH instead LH
	22	Fl1:2 Fl2:4 Fl3:7 Cl:1 Hn:2 Tb:3 Vc:2	13	1	7	21	Pf1 Pf2	14		 5	19	Missing: 2LH, Poss: 1HH instead MH
	23	Fl1:6 Fl3:1 Cl:4 Hn:5 Tp:2 Tb:1 Vc:4 Db:2	7	6	12	25	Pf1 Pf2		7	4 7	18	Missing: 6HH, 1LH, Poss: 1MH instead HH
	24	Fl1:9 Fl2:1 Fl3:4 CL:2 Hn:3 Vc:7	14	2	10	26	Pf1 Pf2	11	5 9	2	27	Extra: 1MH, Poss: 3MH instead HH, 8MH instead LH
	25	Fl2:2 Cl:7 Hn:2 Tp:5 Tb:1 Vc:4 Db:2	2	12	9	23	Pf1 Pf2	7		7 11	25	Extra: 2LH, Poss: 5HH instead MH, 7LH instead MH
	26	Fl1:8 Fl2:5 Fl3:1 Tp:3 Tb:1 Db:4	14	3	5	22	Pf1 Pf2	9 7			16	Missing: 1MH, 5LH, Poss: 1HH instead MH
	27	Fl1:3 Fl3:4 Cl:3 Hn:4 Tb:2 Pf:12 Vc:6 Db:4	12→ 7	→ 5	→ 16	40	Pf1 Pf2	1	7	1 10	19	Missing: 18HH(?), 3LH, Poss: 2MH instead LH

Rehearsal nr.	Ictus	Inst.	HH	MH	LH	Total	Inst.	HH	MH	LH	Total	Discrep.
	28	Fl2:2 Hn:4 Tp:1 Tb:3 Vc:5	2	1	12	15	Pf1 Pf2	14	 5		19	Extra: 4HH, Poss: 8HH instead LH, 4MH instead LH
	29	Fl2:6 Fl3:4 Cl:9 Hn:1 Tp:2 Tb:4 Db:1	10	11	6	27	Pf1 Pf2		10	 9	19	Missing: 7HH, 1MH, Poss: 3LH instead HH
	30	Fl1:4 Fl2:1 Fl3:6 Cl:9 Hn:1 Tp:2 Tb:4 Db:1	11	11	6	28	Pf1 Pf2	6	3 5	5 7	26	Missing: 2HH, Poss: 3LH instead HH, 3LH instead MH
III[8]	31	Fl1:7 Fl3:2 Cl:4 Tb:7 Vc:4 Db:3	9	4	14	27	Pf1 Pf2	7 5		4	16	Missing: 1MH, 10LH, Poss: 3HH instead MH
	32	Fl1:6 Fl2:1 Cl:3 Hn:1 Tp:4 Vc:8	7	7	9	23	Pf1 Pf2	 8		8	16	Missing: 7MH, Poss: 1HH instead MH
	33	Fl1:1 Hn:1 Tp:7 Tb:3 Db:2	1	7	6	14	Pf1	8	3		11	Missing: 3LH, Poss: 4HH instead MH, 3HH instead LH
	34	Fl2:5 Fl3:6 Cl:2 Tp:4 Tb:7 Db:6	11	6	13	30	Pf1 Pf2	 7	7		14	Missing: 3HH, 13LH, Poss: 1MH instead HH

Rehearsal nr.	Ictus	Inst.	HH	MH	LH	Total	Inst.	HH	MH	LH	Total	Discrep.
	35	Fl1:2 Fl2:4 Fl3:6 Hn:5 Tp:1 Tb:4 Vc:3 Db:2	12	1	14	27	Pf1 Pf2	12	 7	 4	23	Missing: 4LH, Poss: 6MH instead LH
	36	Fl2:3 Fl3:1 Cl:2 Hn:1 Tp:4 Tb:2 Vc:9	4	6	12	22	Pf1 Pf2	 9		11	20	Missing: 2MH, Poss: 4HH instead MH, 1HH instead LH
	37	Fl1:5 Fl3:3 Cl:1 Tp:2 Tb:1 Db:3	8	3	4	15	Pf1 Pf2	7	6	 2	15	Poss: 1MH instead HH, 2MH instead LH
	38	Fl1:3 Fl2:2 Fl3:1 Cl:6 Hn:1 Tp:2 Tb:1 Vc:4	6	8	6	20	Pf1 Pf2	9		3 7	19	Missing: 1MH, Poss: 3HH instead MH, 4LH instead MH
	39	Fl1:7 Fl2:6 Fl3:5 Hn:4 Tp:1 Tb:2 Db:1	18	1	7	26	Pf1		13		13	Missing: 12HH, 1LH, Poss: 6MH instead HH, 6MH instead LH
	40	Tp:9		9		9	Pf1 Pf2		5 4		9	none

Discrepancies Page 11:

12 icti none
19 icti with fewer numbers in 2-piano version
3 icti with fewer numbers in ensemble version
0 icti empty in 2-piano version, but not in ensemble version
26 icti with numbers shifted in range.

Rehearsal nr.	Ictus	Inst.	HH	MH	LH	Total	Inst.	HH	MH	LH	Total	Discrep.
IV[8]	1	Empty				0	Empty				0	none
	2	Hn:7 Tp:8 Tb:5 Pf:11	11	→ 8	→ 12	31	P1 P2	11	8 7	5	31	Poss: 7 MH instead LH
	3	Pf:7	7	→	→	7	P1	7			7	None
	4	Empty				0	Empty				0	None
	5	Pf:3 Vc:3	3	→	→ 3	6	P1 P2		5	1	6	Poss: 2MH instead LH
	6	Fl1:4 Tp:2 Vc:2	4	2	2	8	P1 P2	6	2		8	Poss: 2 HH instead MH
	7	Fl3:5 Hn:3 Pf:9 Db:1	9 5	→	→ 4	18	P1 P2		9 2		11	Missing: 5 HH, 2 LH, Poss: 2 MH instead LH
	8	Fl1:2 Fl2:3 Cl:2 Tb:4	5	2	4	11	P1 P2	5		6	11	Poss: 2 LH instead MH
	9	Empty				0	Empty				0	None
	10	Empty				0	Empty				0	None
V[8]	11	Hn:3 Tb:1			4	4	P1 P2		3	1	4	Poss: 3 MH instead LH
	12	Empty				0	Empty				0	None
	13	Empty				0	Empty				0	None
	14	Fl3:6 Cl:3 Hn:4 Tp:5	6	8	4	18	P1 P2	11	4	3	18	Poss: 4 HH instead MH, 1 HH instead LH
	15	Fl1:1 Vc:1	1		1	2	P1 P2		1 1		2	Poss: 1 MH instead HH, 1 MH instead LH
	16	Empty				0	Empty				0	None
	17	Hn:3 Pf:4	4	→	→ 3	7	P1	4	3		7	Poss: 3 MH instead LH
	18	Tb:2			2	2	P1 P2			1 1	2	None
	19	Hn:1 Tp:2 Tb:4		2	5	7	P1 P2		2	1 4	7	None
	20	Fl1:5 Fl2:3 Cl:4	8	4		12	P1 P2	7		5	12	Poss: 1 LH instead HH, 4 LH instead MH
I[9]	21	Fl1:2 Fl3:5 Cl:7	7	7		14	P1 P2	7		7	14	Poss: 7 LH instead MH

Rehearsal nr.	Ictus	Inst.	HH	MH	LH	Total	Inst.	HH	MH	LH	Total	Discrep.
	22	Fl2:4 Fl3:4 Cl:3	8	3		11	P1 P2	4	4	 3	11	Poss: 4 MH instead HH, 3 LH instead MH
	23	Fl1:1 Fl2:2 Fl3:3	6			6	P1 P2	3 3				None
	24	Fl1:6 Fl2:5 Fl3:2	13			13	P1 P2	 6	7		13	Poss: 7 MH instead HH
	25	Fl1:3 Fl2:2	5			5	P1	5				None
	26	Fl2:1 Fl3:3 Cl:2	4	2		6	P1 P2		4	 2	6	Poss: 4 MH instead HH, 2 LH instead MH
	27	Fl1:7 Cl:1	7	1		8	P1 P2	7		 1	8	Poss: 1 LH instead LH
	28	Fl2:6 Fl3:5 Cl:3	11	3		14	P1 P2	 1	9	 3	13	Missing: 1 HH, 9 MH instead HH, 3 LH instead MH
	29	Fl1:4 Fl2:3 Fl3:4	11			11	P1 P2		7 4		11	Poss: 11 MH instead HH
	30	Fl1:1 Fl3:7 Cl:6	8	6		14	P1 P2	 4	 4	6	14	Poss: 4 MH instead HH, 2 LH instead HH, 6 LH instead MH
II[9]	31	Fl1:4 Fl2:2 Fl3;3	9			9	P1 P2	 5	4		9	Poss: 4 MH instead HH
	32	Fl2:1 Fl3:6 Cl:3 Hn:5	7	3	5	15	P1 P2		7 2	 3	12	Missing: 1 MH, 2 LH, Poss: 7 MH instead HH
	33	Fl1:3 Fl2:5 Cl:7 Pf:10	10 8	→ 7	→	25	P1 P2	10		 7	17	Missing: 8 HH
	34	Fl3:4 Hn:3 Tp:6 Db:5	4	6	8	18	P1 P2		8 5		13	Missing: 4 HH, 1 MH, Poss: 8 MH instead LH

Rehearsal nr.	Ictus	Inst.	HH	MH	LH	Total	Inst.	HH	MH	LH	Total	Discrep.
	35	Fl1:2 Fl3:3 Cl:2 Hn:4 Tp:2 Pf:3 Vc:7	3 5	→ 4	→ 11	23	P1 P2	7	4	 5	16	Missing: 1 HH, 6 LH
	36	Fl1:1 Fl2:4 Fl3:5 Cl:6 Tb:3 Vc:2 Db:3	10	6	8	24	P1 P2		 5	9	14	Missing: 10 HH, Poss: 1 LH instead MH
	37	Cl:4 Pf:7	7	→ 4	→	11	P1 P2	7		 4	11	Poss: 4 LH instead MH
	38	Fl1:6 Fl2:5 Fl3:4 CL:3 Pf:2	2 15	→ 3	→	20	P1 P2	 5	8	 3	16	Missing: 4 HH
	39	Fl1:3 Fl2:2	5			5	P1	5			5	None
	40	Fl1:4 Fl2:5 Cl:1	9	1		10	P1 P2		9	 1	10	Poss: 9 MH instead HH, 1 LH instead MH

Discrepancies Page 12:

0 icti none
31 icti with fewer numbers in 2-piano version
2 icti with fewer numbers in ensemble version
25 icti with numbers shifted in range.

Rehearsal nr.	Ictus	Inst.	HH	MH	LH	Total	Inst.	HH	MH	LH	Total	Discrep.
III[9]	1	Fl1:7 Fl2:3 Fl3:2 Cl:4	12	4		16	Pf1 Pf2	7	3	2 4	16	Poss: 5LH instead HH, 1LH instead MH
	2	Fl1:2 Fl2:4 Fl3:7 Cl:4	13	4		17	Pf1 Pf2	2	3 1	7 4	17	Poss: 11LH instead HH
	3	Fl1:1 Fl3:3 Cl:6	4	6		10	Pf1 Pf2	4		 6	10	Poss: 6LH instead MH
	4	Fl1:8 Fl2:6 Fl3:2	16			16	Pf1 Pf2		11 5		16	Poss: 16MH instead HH
	5	Fl1:5 Fl2:2 Cl:7	7	7		14	Pf1 Pf2	7		 7	14	Poss: 7LH instead MH
	6	Fl2:1 Fl3:6 Cl:3 Hn:6	7	3	6	16	Pf1 Pf2	 7	5	3	15	Missing: 1LH, Poss: 2MH instead LH
	7	Fl1:3 Fl2:4 Pf:10	10→ 7	→	→	17	Pf1 Pf2	10	 7		17	Poss: 7MH instead HH
	8	Fl3:6 Cl:2 Hn:3 Tp:6 Db:5	6	8	8	22	Pf1 Pf2	 6	 6	7	19	Missing: 2MH, 1LH
	9	Fl1:2 Fl2:3 Fl3:4 Hn:4 Tp:2 Pf:3 Vc:7	3→ 9	→ 2	→ 11	25	Pf1 Pf2	10 7			17	Missing: 8LH, Poss: 2HH instead MH, 3HH instead LH
	10	Fl1:1 Fl2:3 FL3:6 Cl:5 Vc:2 Db:3	10	5	5	20	Pf1 Pf2		10	 7	17	Missing: 3HH, Poss: 5MH instead HH, 2LH instead HH
IV[9]	11	Fl1:6 Fl2:5 Fl3:8 Cl:7 Tb:3	19	7	3	29	Pf1 Pf2	10	 7		17	Missing: 9HH, 3LH
	12	Fl1:4 Pf:7	7→ 4	→	→	11	Pf1 Pf2	 4		7	11	none

Rehearsal nr.	Ictus	Inst.	HH	MH	LH	Total	Inst.	HH	MH	LH	Total	Discrep.
	13	Fl2:5 Fl3:3 Cl:6 Pf:2	2→ 8	→ 6	→	16	Pf1 Pf2		10	6	16	Poss: 8MH instead HH, 6LH instead MH
	14	Fl1:5 Fl3:6 Cl:4	11	4		15	Pf1 Pf2	10 1		4	15	Poss: 4LH instead MH
	15	Fl1:5 Fl2:6 Fl3:2 Cl:3	13	3		16	Pf1 Pf2		10 3	3	16	Poss: 10MH instead HH, 3LH instead HH
	16	Fl1:4 Fl2:4 Fl3:7 Cl:2	15	2		17	Pf1 Pf2	4	4 7	2	17	Poss: 9MH instead HH, 2LH instead HH
	17	Fl2:6 Fl3:1 Cl:6	7	6		13	Pf1 Pf2		7	6	13	Poss: 1MH instead HH, 6LH instead HH
	18	Fl2:2 Fl3:3 CL:4	7	4		11	Pf1 Pf2	5		4	9	Missing: 2HH, Poss: 4LH instead MH
	19	Fl1:5 Fl3:2	7			7	Pf2		7		7	Poss: 7MH instead HH
	20	Fl3:7	7			7	Pf1	7			7	none
V^{9}	21	Fl2:6 Cl:3	6	3		9	Pf1 Pf2		6	3	9	Poss: 3MH instead HH, 3LH instead HH
	22	Fl1:7 Fl2:4 Fl3:5 Cl:1	16	1		17	Pf1 Pf2	11	5	1	17	Poss: 4MH instead HH, 1LH instead HH
	23	Fl1:3 Cl:2	3	2		5	Pf2	3		2	5	Poss: 2LH instead MH
	24	Fl1:7 Fl2:8 Fl3:5 Cl:4	20	4		24	Pf1 Pf2		13 7	4	24	Poss: 16MH instead HH, 4LH instead HH
	25	Fl1:4 Fl2:3 Fl3:2	9			9	Pf1 Pf2	5 4			9	none
	26	Fl1:2 Fl2:7 Fl3:3	12			12	Pf1 Pf2	3	9		12	Poss: 9MH instead HH
	27	Fl1:1 Fl3:6 Cl:3 Hn:5	7	3	5	15	Pf1 Pf2	11	3	5	19	Extra: 4HH

Rehearsal nr.	Ictus	Inst.	HH	MH	LH	Total	Inst.	HH	MH	LH	Total	Discrep.
	28	Cl:4 Pf:10	10→	→ 4	→	14	Pf1 Pf2		8	 6	14	none
	29	Fl1:8 Fl2:6 Fl3:7 Hn:3 Tp:6 Db:5	21	6	8	35	Pf1 Pf2	13 6	 3		22	Missing: 2HH, 3MH, 8LH
	30	Fl2:3 Fl3:4 Cl:7 Hn:4 Tp:2 Pf:3 Vc:7	3→ 7	→ 9	→ 11	30	Pf1 Pf2	3	4 7	7	21	Missing: 4HH, 5LH
I[10]	31	Fl1:5 Fl2:2 Fl3:7 Tb:3 Vc:2 Db:3	14		8	22	Pf1 Pf2	7 5	 2	3 3	20	Missing: 2HH, Poss: 2MH instead LH
	32	Fl1:3 Fl2:4 Fl3:3 CL:2 Pf:7	7→ 10	→ 2	→	19	Pf1 Pf2		10	 2	12	Missing: 7HH, Poss: 3MH instead HH
	33	Fl1:2 Fl2:1 Fl3:5 Cl:1 Pf:2	2→ 8	→ 1	→	11	Pf1 Pf2	7		 3	10	Missing: 1HH, Poss: 2LH instead HH, 1LH instead MH
	34	Fl1:1 Fl2:3 Cl:6 Hn:5	4	6	5	15	Pf1 Pf2		9	 6	15	Poss: 3MH instead HH, 1LH instead HH
	35	Fl1:4 Fl3:6 Cl:4 Pf:10	10→ 10	→ 4	→	24	Pf1 Pf2	6	7 5	1 3	22	Missing: 2HH, Poss: 2MH instead HH
	36	Fl2:5 Fl3:3 Hn:3 Tp:6 Db:5	8	6	8	22	Pf1 Pf2		8 5		13	Missing: 1HH, 8LH, Poss: 7MH instead HH

Rehearsal nr.	Ictus	Inst.	HH	MH	LH	Total	Inst.	HH	MH	LH	Total	Discrep.
	37	Fl1:2 Fl2:7 Fl3:4 Cl:3 Hn:4 Tp:2 Pf:3 Vc:7	3→ 13	→ 5	→ 11	32	Pf1 Pf2	2 7	4	4 2	19	Missing: 4HH, 1MH, 8LH(?)
	38	Fl2:6 Fl3:7 Cl:5 Tb:3 Vc:2 Db:3	13	5	8	26	Pf1 Pf2		13 5	 3	21	Missing: 5LH, Poss: 13MH instead HH
	39	Fl1:4 Fl2:2 Cl:4 Pf:7	7→ 6	→ 4	→	17	Pf1 Pf2	13		 4	17	Poss: 4LH instead MH
	40	Fl1:7 Fl2:3 Fl3:6 Pf:2	2→ 16	→	→	18	Pf1 Pf2	 9	9		18	Poss: 7MH instead HH

Discrepancies Page 13:

4 icti none
15 icti with fewer numbers in 2-piano version
1 ictus with fewer numbers in ensemble version
0 icti empty in 2-piano version, but not in ensemble version
30 icti with numbers shifted in range.

Rehearsal nr.	Ictus	Inst.	HH	MH	LH	Total	Inst.	HH	MH	LH	Total	Discrep.
II[10]	1	Fl1:5 Fl3:4 Cl:6	9	6		15	Pf1 Pf2	9		 6	15	Poss: 6LH instead MH
	2	Fl1:8 Fl2:4 Fl3:5 Cl:2	17	2		19	Pf1 Pf2		9 10		19	Poss: 17MH instead HH
	3	Fl1:3 Fl2:5 Cl:1	8	1		9	Pf1 Pf2	3	5	 1	9	Poss: 4MH instead HH, 1LH instead HH
	4	Fl1:1 Fl2:6 Fl3:5 Cl:7	12	7		19	Pf1 Pf2	10 1	 1	 7	19	Poss: 1MH instead HH, 7 LH instead MH
	5	Fl1:2 Fl2:4 Fl3:3	9			9	Pf1 Pf2	 1	6 1	 1	9	Poss: 7MH instead HH, 1LH instead HH
	6	Fl1:7 Fl2:6 Fl3:4 Cl:8	17	8		25	Pf1 Pf2	6	7	4 8	25	Poss: 11LH instead HH, 1LH instead MH
	7	Fl1:5 Fl2:3 Cl:4	8	4		12	Pf1	7			7	Missing: 1HH, 4MH
	8	Fl1:2 Fl3:5 Cl:7	7	7		14	Pf1 Pf2	7		 7	14	Poss: 7LH instead MH
	9	Fl2:4 Fl3:4 Cl:3	8	3		11	Pf1 Pf2	4	4	 3	11	Poss: 4MH instead HH, 3LH instead MH
	10	Fl1:1 Fl2:2 FL3:3	6			6	Pf1 Pf2	3 3			6	none
III[10]	11	Fl1:6 Fl2:5 Fl3:2	13			13	Pf1 Pf2	 6	7		13	Poss: 7MH instead HH
	12	Fl1:3 Fl2:2	5			5	Pf1	5			5	none
	13	Fl2:1 Fl3:3 Cl:2	4	2		6	Pf1 Pf2		4	 2	6	Poss: 4MH instead HH, 2LH instead MH
	14	Fl1:7 Cl:1	7	1		8	Pf1 Pf2	7		 1	8	Poss: 1LH instead MH

Rehearsal nr.	Ictus	Inst.	HH	MH	LH	Total	Inst.	HH	MH	LH	Total	Discrep.
	15	Fl2:6 Fl3:5 Cl:3	11	3		14	Pf1 Pf2	 1	9	 3	13	Missing: 1HH, Poss: 9MH instead HH, 3 LH instead MH
	16	Fl1:4 Fl2:3 Fl3:4	11			11	Pf1 Pf2		7 4		11	Poss: 11MH instead HH
	17	Fl1:1 Fl3:7 CL:6	8	6		14	Pf1 Pf2	 4	 4	6	14	Poss: 4MH instead HH, 6LH instad MH
	18	Fl1:4 Fl2:2 Fl3:3	9			9	Pf1 Pf2	 5	4		9	Poss: 4MH instead HH
	19	Fl2:1 Fl3:6 Cl:3 Hn:5	7	3	5	15	Pf1 Pf2		7 2	 3	12	Missing: 1HH, 2LH, Poss: 6MH instead HH
	20	Fl1:3 Fl2:5 Cl:7 Pf:10	10→ 8	→ 7	→	25	Pf1 Pf2	10		 7	17	Missing: 8HH, Poss: 7LH instead MH
IV[10]	21	Fl3:4 Hn:3 Tp:6 Db:5	4	6	8	18	Pf1 Pf2		8 5		13	Missing: 4HH, 1LH, Poss: 7MH instead LH
	22	Fl1:2 Fl3:3 CL:2 Hn:4 Tp:2 Pf:3 Vc:7	3→ 5	→ 4	→ 11	23	Pf1 Pf2	7	4	 5	16	Missing: 7LH
	23	Fl1:1 Fl2:4 Fl3:5 Cl:6 Tb:3 Vc:2 Db:3	10	6	8	24	Pf1 Pf2		 5	9	14	Missing: 10HH, Poss: 1LH instead MH
	24	Cl:4 Pf:7	7→	→ 4	→	11	Pf1 Pf2	7		 4	11	Poss: 4LH instead MH
	25	Fl1:6 Fl2:5 Fl3:4 Cl:3 Pf:2	2→ 15	→ 3	→	20	Pf1 Pf2	 5	8	 3	16	Missing: 4HH, Poss: 6MH instead HH, 3LH instead MH
	26	Fl1:3 Fl3:2	5			5	Pf1	5			5	none

Rehearsal nr.	Ictus	Inst.	HH	MH	LH	Total	Inst.	HH	MH	LH	Total	Discrep.
	27	Fl1:4 Fl2:5 CL:1	9	1		10	Pf1 Pf2		9	 1	10	Poss: 9MH instead HH, 1LH instead MH
	28	Fl1:7 Fl2:3 Fl3:2 Cl:4	12	4		16	Pf1 Pf2	7	3 1	2 4	17	Extra: 1LH, Poss: 5LH instead HH
	29	Fl1:2 Fl2:4 Fl3:7 Cl:4	13	4		17	Pf1 Pf2	2	3 1	7 4	17	Poss: 11LH instead HH
	30	Fl1:1 Fl3:3 CL:6	4	6		10	Pf1 Pf2	4		 6	10	Poss: 6LH instead MH
V[10]	31	Fl1:8 Fl2:6 Fl3:2	16			16	Pf1 Pf2		11 5		16	Poss: 16MH instead HH
	32	Fl1:5 Fl2:2 Cl:7	7	7		14	Pf1 Pf2	7		 7	14	Poss: 7LH instead MH
	33	Fl2:1 Fl3:6 CL:3 Hn:5	7	3	5	15	Pf1 Pf2	 7	5	3	15	Poss: 2MH instead LH
	34	Fl1:3 Fl2:4 Pf:10	10→ 7	→	→	17	Pf1 Pf2	10	 7		17	Poss: 7MH instead HH
	35	Fl3:6 Cl:2 Hn:3 Tp:6 Db:5	6	8	8	22	Pf1 Pf2	 6	 6	7	19	Missing: 2MH, 1LH
	36	Fl1:2 Fl2:3 Fl3:4 Hn:4 Tp:2 Pf:3 Vc:7	3→ 9	→ 2	→ 11	25	Pf1 Pf2	10 7			17	Missing: 8LH, Poss: 2HH instead MH, 3HH instead LH
	37	Fl1:1 Fl2:3 Fl3:6 Cl:5 Vc:2 Db:3	10	5	5	20	Pf1 Pf2		10	 7	17	Missing: 3HH, Poss: 5MH instead HH, 2LH instead HH

Rehearsal nr.	Ictus	Inst.	HH	MH	LH	Total	Inst.	HH	MH	LH	Total	Discrep.
	38	Fl1:6 Fl2:5 Fl3:8 Cl:7 Tb:3	19	7	3	29	Pf1 Pf2	10	7		17	Missing: 9HH, 3LH
	39	Fl1:4 Pf:7	7→ 4	→	→	11	Pf1 Pf2	4		7	11	none
	40	Fl2:5 Fl3:3 Cl:6 Pf:2	2→ 8	→ 6	→	16	Pf1 Pf2		10	6	16	Poss: 2MH instead HH, 6LH instead HH

Discrepancies Page 14:

4 icti none
12 icti with fewer numbers in 2-piano version
1 ictus with fewer numbers in ensemble version
0 icti empty in 2-piano version, but not in ensemble version
33 icti with numbers shifted in range.

Rehearsal nr.	Ictus	Inst.	HH	MH	LH	Total	Inst.	HH	MH	LH	Total	Discrep.
I[11]	1	Fl1:5 Fl3:6 Cl:4	11	4		15	Pf1 Pf2	10 1		 4	15	Poss: 4LH instead MH
	2	Fl1:5 Fl2:6 Fl3:2 Cl:3	13	3		16	Pf1 Pf2		10 3	 3	16	Poss: 10MH instead HH, 3LH instead HH
	3	Fl1:4 Fl2:4 Fl3:7 Cl:2	15	2		17	Pf1 Pf2	4	4 7	 2	17	Poss: 11MH instead HH, 2LH instead MH
	4	Fl2:6 Fl3:1 Cl:6	7	6		13	Pf1 Pf2		7	 6	13	Poss: 7MH instead HH, 6LH instead MH
	5	Fl2:2 Fl3:3 Cl:4	5	4		9	Pf1 Pf2	 5		4	9	Poss: 4LH instead MH
	6	Fl1:5 Fl3:2	7			7	Pf2		7		7	Poss: 7MH instead HH
	7	Fl3:7	7			7	Pf1	7			7	none
	8	Fl2:6 Cl:3	6	3		9	Pf1 Pf2		6	 3	9	Poss: 6MH instead HH, 3LH instead MH
	9	Fl1:7 Fl2:8 Fl3:5 Cl:4	20	4		24	Pf1 Pf2	11	 5	 1	17	Missing: 7HH, Poss: 1MH instead HH, 1LH instead HH
	10	Fl1:3 Cl:2	3	2		5	Pf2	3		2	5	Poss: 2LH instead MH
II[11]	11	Fl1:7 Fl2:8 Fl3:5 Cl:4	20	4		24	Pf1 Pf2		13 7	 4	24	Poss: 20MH instead HH, 4LH instead MH
	12	Fl1:4 Fl2:3 Fl3:2	9			9	Pf1 Pf2	5 4			9	none
	13	Fl1:2 Fl2:7 Fl3:3	12			12	Pf1 Pf2	 3	9		12	Poss: 9MH instead HH
	14	Fl1:1 Fl3:6 Cl:3 Hn:5	7	3	5	15	Pf1 Pf2	11	 3	 5	19	Extra: 7HH
	15	Cl:4 Pf:10	10→	→ 4	→	14	Pf1 Pf2		8	 6	14	none

Rehearsal nr.	Ictus	Inst.	HH	MH	LH	Total	Inst.	HH	MH	LH	Total	Discrep.
	16	Fl1:8 Fl2:6 Fl3:7 Hn:3 Tp:6 Db:5	21	6	8	35	Pf1 Pf2	13 6	3		22	Missing: 2HH, 3MH, 8LH
	17	Fl2:3 Fl3:4 Cl:7 Hn:4 Tp:2 Pf:3 Vc:7	3→ 7	→ 9	→ 11	30	Pf1 Pf2	3	4 7	7	21	Missing: 7HH, 2LH, Poss: 2MH instead LH
	18	Fl1:5 Fl2:2 Fl3:7 Tb:3 Vc:2 Db:3	14		8	22	Pf1 Pf2	7 5	 2	3 3	20	Missing: 2HH, Poss: 2MH instead LH
	19	Fl1:3 Fl2:4 Fl3:3 Cl:2 Pf:7	7→ 10	→ 2	→	19	Pf1 Pf2		10	 2	12	Missing: 7HH(?), Poss: 10MH instead HH, 2 LH instead MH
	20	Fl1:2 Fl2:1 Fl3:5 Cl:1 Pf:2	2→ 8	→ 1	→	11	Pf1 Pf2	7		 3	10	Missing: 1HH, Poss: 1LH instead MH
III[11]	21	Fl1:1 Fl2:3 Cl:6 Hn:5	4	6	5	15	Pf1 Pf2		9	 6	15	Poss: 3MH instead HH, 1LH instead HH
	22	Fl1:4 Fl3:6 Cl:4 Pf:10	10→ 10	→ 4	→	24	Pf1 Pf2	6	7 5	1 3	22	Missing: 2HH
	23	Fl2:5 Fl3:3 Hn:3 Tp:6 Db:5	8	6	8	22	Pf1 Pf2		8 5		13	Missing: 8HH, 1LH, Poss: 7MH instead LH

Rehearsal nr.	Ictus	Inst.	HH	MH	LH	Total	Inst.	HH	MH	LH	Total	Discrep.
	24	Fl1:2 Fl2:7 Fl3:4 Cl:3 Hn:4 Tp:2 Pf:3 Vc:7	3→ 13	→ 5	→ 11	32	Pf1 Pf2	2 7	4	4 2	19	Missing: 4HH, 1MH, 8LH(?)
	25	Fl2:6 Fl3:7 Cl:5 Tb:3 Vc:2 Db:3	13	5	8	26	Pf1 Pf2		13 5	 3	21	Missing: 5LH, Poss: 13MH instead HH
	26	Fl1:4 Fl2:2 Cl:4 Pf:7	7→ 6	→ 4	→	17	Pf1 Pf2	13		 4	17	Poss: 4MH instead LH
	27	Fl1:7 Fl2:3 Fl3:6 Pf:2	2→ 16	→	→	18	Pf1 Pf2	 9	9		18	Poss: 7MH instead HH
	28	Fl1:5 Fl3:4 Cl:6	9	6		15	Pf1 Pf2	9		 6	15	Poss: 6LH instead MH
	29	Fl1:8 Fl2:4 Fl3:5 Cl:2	17	2		19	Pf1 Pf2		9 10		19	Poss: 17MH instead HH
	30	Fl1:3 Fl2:5 Cl:1	8	1		9	Pf1 Pf2	3	5	 1	9	Poss: 5MH instead HH, 1 LH instead MH
IV[11]	31	Fl1:1 Fl2:6 Fl3:5 Cl:7	12	7		19	Pf1 Pf2	10 1	 1	 7	19	Poss: 1MH instead HH, 7LH instead MH
	32	Fl1:2 Fl2:4 Fl3:3	9			9	Pf1 Pf2	 1	6 1	 1	9	Poss: 7MH instead HH, 1LH instead HH
	33	Fl1:7 Fl2:6 Fl3:4 Cl:8	17	8		25	Pf1 Pf2	6	7	4 8	25	Poss: 11LH instead HH, 1LH instead MH
	34	Cl:4 Pf:3	3→	→ 4	→	7	Pf1			7	7	Poss: 4LH instead MH
	35	Cl:2 Pf:1	1→	→ 2	→	3	Pf2			3	3	Poss: 2LH instead MH

Rehearsal nr.	Ictus	Inst.	HH	MH	LH	Total	Inst.	HH	MH	LH	Total	Discrep.
	36	Pf:4	4→	→	→	4	Pf1 Pf2		3	1	4	none
	37	Cl:5 Pf:2	5→	→ 2	→	7	Pf1 Pf2			5 2	7	Poss: 2LH instead MH
	38	Cl:3		3		3	Pf1 Pf2		1	1 1	3	Poss: 2LH instead MH
	39	Cl:6 Pf:1	1→	→ 6	→	7	Pf1			7	7	Poss: 6LH instead MH
	40	Cl:4 Pf:3	3→	→ 4	→	7	Pf1			7	7	Poss: 4LH instead MH

Discrepancies Page 15:

4 icti none
10 icti with fewer numbers in 2-piano version
1 ictus with fewer numbers in ensemble version
0 icti empty in 2-piano version, but not in ensemble version
32 icti with numbers shifted in range.

Rehearsal nr.	Ictus	Inst.	HH	MH	LH	Total	Inst.	HH	MH	LH	Total	Discrep.
V[11]	1	Fl1:2 Tp:2 Db:2	2	2	2	6	Pf1	4	2		6	Poss: 2HH instead LH
	2	Cl:2 Tb:4		2	4	6	Pf1			6	6	Poss: 2LH instead MH
	3	Cl:1		1		1	Pf2			1	1	Poss: 1LH instead MH
	4	Cl:3 Tb:2		3	2	5	Pf1			5	5	Poss: 3LH instead MH
	5	Cl:4		4		4	Pf1 Pf2			2 2	4	Poss: 4LH instead MH
	6	Tb:4			4	4	Pf1 Pf2			3 1	4	none
	7	Cl:5 Tb:2		5	2	7	Pf1 Pf2		 2	5 	7	Poss: 3LH instead MH
	8	Cl:7 Tb:5		7	5	12	Pf1 Pf2		7 	 5	12	none
	9	Fl1:2 Db:2	2		2	4	Pf1 Pf2	2 	 1	 1	4	Poss: 1MH instead LH
	10	Cl:1 Tb:3 Pf:7 Vc:5	7→	→ 1	→ 8	16	Pf1 Pf2	5		7 4	16	Poss: 1LH instead MH
I[12]	11	Empty				0	Empty				0	none
	12	Cl:4 Tb:3		4	3	7	Pf1			7	7	Poss: 4LH instead MH
	13	Cl:2 Tb:1		2	1	3	Pf2			3	3	Poss: 2LH instead MH
	14	Tb:4			4	4	Pf1 Pf2		 3	1 	4	Poss: 3MH instead LH
	15	Cl:5 Tb:2		5	2	7	Pf1 Pf2			5 2	7	Poss: 5LH instead MH
	16	Cl:3		3		3	Pf1 Pf2		1 	1 1	3	Poss: 2LH instead MH
	17	Cl:6 Tb:1		6	1	7	Pf1			7	7	Poss: 6LH instead MH
	18	Cl:4 TB:3		4	3	7	Pf1			7	7	Poss: 4LH instead MH
	19	Fl1:2 Tp:2 Db:2	2	2	2	6	Pf1	4	2		6	Poss: 2HH instead LH
	20	Cl:2 Tb:4		2	4	6	Pf1			6	6	Poss: 2LH instead MH
II[12]	21	Cl:1		1		1	Pf2			1	1	Poss: 1LH instead MH
	22	Cl:3 Tb:2		3	2	5	Pf1			5	5	Poss: 3LH instead MH
	23	Cl:4		4		4	Pf1 Pf2			2 2	4	Poss: 4LH instead MH

Rehearsal nr.	Ictus	Inst.	HH	MH	LH	Total	Inst.	HH	MH	LH	Total	Discrep.
	24	Tb:4			4	4	Pf1 Pf2			3 1	4	none
	25	Cl:5 Tb:2		5	2	7	Pf1 Pf2		 2	5	7	Poss: 3LH instead MH
	26	Cl:7 Tb:5		7	5	12	Pf1 Pf2		7	 5	12	none
	27	Db:2			2	2	Pf1 Pf2	2	 1	 1	4	Extra: 2HH, Poss: 1MH instead LH
	28	Cl:1 Tb:3 Pf:7 Vc:5	7→	→ 1	→ 8	16	Pf1 Pf2	5		7 4	16	Poss: 1LH instead MH
	29	Empty				0	Empty				0	none
	30	Fl1:1 Fl2:1 Fl3:1 Cl:1 Hn:1 Tp:1 Tb:1 Pf:1 Vc:1 Db:1	1→ 3	→ 2	→ 4	10	Pf1 Pf2	2 1	1 1	2 1	8	Missing: 3LH(?)
III[12]	31	Fl1:1 Fl2:1 Fl3:1 Cl:1 Hn:1 Tp:1 Tb:1 Pf:1 Vc:1 Db:1	1→ 3	→ 2	→ 4	10	Pf1 Pf2	5 1	5 1	 1	13	Extra: 3HH(?), Poss: 3MH instead LH
	32	Fl1:1 Fl2:1 Fl3:1 Cl:1 Hn:1 Tp:1 Tb:1 Pf:1 Vc:1 Db:1	1→ 3	→ 2	→ 4	10	Pf1 Pf2	 1	5 1	5 1	13	Extra: 2LH, 1MH, Poss: 2MH instead HH

Rehearsal nr.	Ictus	Inst.	HH	MH	LH	Total	Inst.	HH	MH	LH	Total	Discrep.
	33	Fl1:1 Fl2:1 Fl3:1 Cl:1 Hn:1 Tp:1 Tb:1 Pf:1 Vc:1 Db:1	1→ 3	→ 2	→ 4	10	Pf1 Pf2	5 1	 1	5 1	13	Extra: 3HH, Poss: 1LH instead MH
	34	Fl1:1 Fl2:1 Fl3:1 Cl:1 Hn:1 Tp:1 Tb:1 Pf:1 Vc:1 Db:1	1→ 3	→ 2	→ 4	10	Pf1 Pf2	3 1	5 1	2 1	13	Extra: 3MH, Poss: 1LH instead MH
	35	Fl1:1 Fl2:1 Fl3:1 Cl:1 Hn:1 Tp:1 Tb:1 Pf:1 Vc:1 Db:1	1→ 3	→ 2	→ 4	10	Pf1 Pf2	7 1	1 1	2 1	13	Extra: 3HH, Poss: 1LH instead HH
	36	Fl1:1 Fl2:1 Fl3:1 Cl:1 Hn:1 Tp:1 Tb:1 Pf:1 Vc:1 Db:1	1→ 3	→ 2	→ 4	10	Pf1 Pf2	2 1	7 1	1 1	13	Extra: 3MH, Poss: 2LH instead MH
	37	Fl1:1 Fl2:1 Fl3:1 Cl:1 Hn:1 Tp:1 Tb:1 Pf:1 Vc:1 Db:1	1→ 3	→ 2	→ 4	10	Pf1 Pf2	5 1	5 1	 1	13	Extra: 3HH, Poss: 3MH instead LH

Rehearsal nr.	Ictus	Inst.	HH	MH	LH	Total	Inst.	HH	MH	LH	Total	Discrep.
	38	Empty				0	Empty				0	none
	39	Empty				0	Empty				0	none
	40	Tb:3 Pf:7 Vc:5	7→	→	→ 8	15	Pf1 Pf2	7	5	3	15	Poss: 5Mh instead LH

Discrepancies Page 16:

8 icti none
1 ictus with fewer numbers in 2-piano version
8 icti with fewer numbers in ensemble version
0 icti empty in 2-piano version, but not in ensemble version
31 icti with numbers shifted in range.

Rehearsal nr.	Ictus	Inst.	HH	MH	LH	Total	Inst.	HH	MH	LH	Total	Discrep.
IV[12]	1	Empty				0	Empty				0	none
	2	Empty				0	Empty				0	none
	3	Empty				0	Empty				0	none
	4	Empty				0	Empty				0	none
	5	Empty				0	Empty				0	none
	6	Fl1:1 Fl2:1 Fl3:1 Cl:1 Hn:1 Tp:1 Tb:1 Pf:1 Vc:1 Db:1	1→ 3	→ 2	→ 4	10	Pf1 Pf2	5 1	5 1	 1	13	Extra: 3HH, Poss: 3MH instead LH
	7	Fl1:1 Fl2:1 Fl3:1 Cl:1 Hn:1 Tp:1 Tb:1 Pf:1 Vc:1 Db:1	1→ 3	→ 2	→ 4	10	Pf1 Pf2	5 1	5 1	 1	13	Extra: 3HH, Poss: 3MH instead LH
	8	Fl1:1 Fl2:1 Fl3:1 Cl:1 Hn:1 Tp:1 Tb:1 Pf:1 Vc:1 Db:1	1→ 3	→ 2	→ 4	10	Pf1 Pf2	5 1	5 1	 1	13	Extra: 3HH, Poss: 3MH instead LH
	9	Fl1:1 Fl2:1 Fl3:1 Cl:1 Hn:1 Tp:1 Tb:1 Pf:1 Vc:1 Db:1	1→ 3	→ 2	→ 4	10	Pf1 Pf2	5	5	 3	13	Extra: 1HH, 2MH, Poss: 1LH instead MH

Rehearsal nr.	Ictus	Inst.	HH	MH	LH	Total	Inst.	HH	MH	LH	Total	Discrep.
	10	Fl1:1 Fl2:1 Fl3:1 Cl:1 Hn:1 Tp:1 Tb:1 Pf:1 Vc:1 Db:1	1→ 3	→ 2	→ 4	10	Pf1 Pf2	5 1	5 1	 1	13	Extra: 3HH, Poss: 3MH instead LH
V[12]	11	Fl1:1 Fl2:1 Fl3:1 Cl:1 Hn:1 Tp:1 Tb:1 Pf:1 Vc:1 Db:1	1→ 3	→ 2	→ 4	10	Pf1 Pf2	5	5 3		13	Extra: 2HH, 1MH, Poss: 4MH instead LH
	12	Fl1:1 Fl2:1 Fl3:1 Cl:1 Hn:1 Tp:1 Tb:1 Pf:1 Vc:1 Db:1	1→ 3	→ 2	→ 4	10	Pf1 Pf2	5 1	5 1	 1	13	Extra: 3HH, Poss: 3MH instead LH
	13	Fl1:1 Fl2:1 Fl3:1 Cl:1 Hn:1 Tp:1 Tb:1 Pf:1 Vc:1 Db:1	1→ 3	→ 2	→ 4	10	Pf1 Pf2	5 1	5 1	 1	13	Extra: 3HH, Poss: 3MH instead LH
	14	Fl1:1 Fl2:1 Fl3:1 Cl:1 Hn:1 Tp:1 Tb:1 Pf:1 Vc:1 Db:1	1→ 3	→ 2	→ 4	10	Pf1 Pf2	5 1		5 2	13	Extra: 3HH, Poss: 2LH instead MH

Rehearsal nr.	Ictus	Inst.	HH	MH	LH	Total	Inst.	HH	MH	LH	Total	Discrep.
	15	Fl1:1 Fl2:1 Fl3:1 Cl:1 Hn:1 Tp:1 Tb:1 Pf:1 Vc:1 Db:1	1→ 3	→ 2	→ 4	10	Pf1 Pf2		5 2	5 1	13	Extra: 3MH(?), Poss: 3LH instead HH
	16	Fl1:1 Fl2:1 Fl3:1 Cl:1 Hn:1 Tp:1 Tb:1 Pf:1 Vc:1 Db:1	1→ 3	→ 2	→ 4	10	Pf1 Pf2	5 1	5	 2	13	Extra: 3HH, Poss: 2MH instead LH
	17	Fl1:1 Fl2:1 Fl3:1 Cl:1 Hn:1 Tp:1 Tb:1 Pf:1 Vc:1 Db:1	1→ 3	→ 2	→ 4	10	Pf1 Pf2	5	5 3		13	Extra: 2HH, 1MH, Poss: 4MH instead LH
	18	Fl1:1 Fl2:1 Fl3:1 Cl:1 Hn:1 Tp:1 Tb:1 Pf:1 Vc:1 Db:1	1→ 3	→ 2	→ 4	10	Pf1 Pf2	5 1	5 1	 1	13	Extra: 3HH, Poss: 3MH instead LH
	19	Empty				0	Empty				0	none
	20	Empty				0	Empty				0	none

Rehearsal nr.	Ictus	Inst.	HH	MH	LH	Total	Inst.	HH	MH	LH	Total	Discrep.
I[13]	21	Tbn:3 Pf:7 Vc:5	7→	→	→ 8	15	Pf1 Pf2	12		 3	15	Poss: 5HH instead LH
	22	Fl1:1 Fl2:1 Fl3:1 Cl:1 Hn:1 Tp:1 Tb:1 Pf:1 Vc:1 Db:1	1→ 3	→ 2	→ 4	10	Pf1 Pf2	 1	7 1	 1	10	Poss: 3MH instead HH, 3MH instead LH
	23	Fl1:1 Fl2:1 Fl3:1 Cl:1 Hn:1 Tp:1 Tb:1 Pf:1 Vc:1 Db:1	1→ 3	→ 2	→ 4	10	Pf1 Pf2	5	 2	1 2	10	Poss: 1HH instead LH
	24	Fl1:1 Fl2:1 Fl3:1 Cl:1 Hn:1 Tp:1 Tb:1 Pf:1 Vc:1 Db:1	1→ 3	→ 2	→ 4	10	Pf1 Pf2	6 1		 3	10	Poss: 2HH instead MH, 1MH instead LH
	25	Fl1:1 Fl2:1 Fl3:1 Cl:1 Hn:1 Tp:1 Tb:1 Pf:1 Vc:1 Db:1	1→ 3	→ 2	→ 4	10	Pf1 Pf2	 1	8 1		10	Poss: 3MH instead HH, 4MH instead LH

Rehearsal nr.	Ictus	Inst.	HH	MH	LH	Total	Inst.	HH	MH	LH	Total	Discrep.
	26	Fl1:1 Fl2:1 Fl3:1 Cl:1 Hn:1 Tp:1 Tb:1 Pf:1 Vc:1 Db:1	1→ 3	→ 2	→ 4	10	Pf1 Pf2	9		 1	10	Poss: 2HH instead MH, 3MH instead LH
	27	Fl1:1 Fl2:1 Fl3:1 Cl:1 Hn:1 Tp:1 Tb:1 Pf:1 Vc:1 Db:1	1→ 3	→ 2	→ 4	10	Pf1 Pf2		 7	3	10	Poss: 3MH instead HH, 1MH instead LH
	28	Fl1:1 Fl2:1 Fl3:1 Cl:1 Hn:1 Tp:1 Tb:1 Pf:1 Vc:1 Db:1	1→ 3	→ 2	→ 4	10	Pf1 Pf2	4 6			10	Poss: 2HH instead MH, 4HH instead LH
	29	Fl1:1 Fl2:1 Fl3:1 Cl:1 Hn:1 Tp:1 Tb:1 Pf:1 Vc:1 Db:1	1→ 3	→ 2	→ 4	10	Pf1		10		10	Poss: 3MH instead HH, 4MH instead LH
	30	Fl1:1 Fl2:1 Fl3:1 Cl:1 Hn:1 Tp:1 Tb:1 Pf:1 Vc:1 Db:1	1→ 3	→ 2	→ 4	10	Pf1 Pf2	8 2			10	Poss: 2HH instead MH, 4HH instead LH

Rehearsal nr.	Ictus	Inst.	HH	MH	LH	Total	Inst.	HH	MH	LH	Total	Discrep.
II[13]	31	Fl1:1 Fl2:1 Fl3:1 Cl:1 Hn:1 Tp:1 Tb:1 Pf:1 Vc:1 Db:1	1→ 3	→ 2	→ 4	10	Pf1 Pf2		 5	5	10	Poss: 3MH instead HH,
	32	Fl1:1 Fl2:1 Fl3:1 Cl:1 Hn:1 Tp:1 Tb:1 Pf:1 Vc:1 Db:1	1→ 3	→ 2	→ 4	10	Pf1 Pf2	5 4		 1	10	Poss: 2HH instead MH, 2HH instead LH
	33	Fl1:1 Fl2:1 Fl3:1 Cl:1 Hn:1 Tp:1 Tb:1 Pf:1 Vc:1 Db:1	1→ 3	→ 2	→ 4	10	Pf1 Pf2	7 1	 1	 1	10	Poss: 1HH instead MH, 3HH instead LH
	34	Fl1:1 Fl2:1 Fl3:1 Cl:1 Hn:1 Tp:1 Tb:1 Pf:1 Vc:1 Db:1	1→ 3	→ 2	→ 4	10	Pf1 Pf2		4 2	4	10	Poss: 3MH instead HH
	35	Fl1:1 Fl2:1 Fl3:1 Cl:1 Hn:1 Tp:1 Tb:1 Pf:1 Vc:1 Db:1	1→ 3	→ 2	→ 4	10	Pf1 Pf2		7	3	10	Poss: 3MH instead HH, 1MH instead LH

Rehearsal nr.	Ictus	Inst.	HH	MH	LH	Total	Inst.	HH	MH	LH	Total	Discrep.
	36	Fl1:1 Fl2:1 Fl3:1 Cl:1 Hn:1 Tp:1 Tb:1 Pf:1 Vc:1 Db:1	1→ 3	→ 2	→ 4	10	Pf1 Pf2	6		3 1	10	Poss: 2HH instead MH
	37	Fl1:1 Fl2:1 Fl3:1 Cl:1 Hn:1 Tp:1 Tb:1 Pf:1 Vc:1 Db:1	1→ 3	→ 2	→ 4	10	Pf1 Pf2	 5	5		10	Poss: 1HH Instead LH, 3MH instead LH
	38	Fl1:1 Fl2:1 Fl3:1 Cl:1 Hn:1 Tp:1 Tb:1 Pf:1 Vc:1 Db:1	1→ 3	→ 2	→ 4	10	Pf1	6	3	1	10	Poss: 2HH instead LH, 1MH instead LH
	39	Fl1:5 Fl3:7 Pf:9	9→ 12	→	→	21	Pf1 Pf2	14	 7		21	none
	40	Fl1:4 Fl3:2 Tp:2	5	2		7	Pf1		8		8	Extra: 1MH, Poss: 5MH instead HH

Discrepancies Page 17:

8 icti none
0 icti with fewer numbers in 2-piano version
14 icti with fewer numbers in ensemble version
0 icti empty in 2-piano version, but not in ensemble version
32 icti with numbers shifted in range.

Rehearsal nr.	Ictus	Inst.	HH	MH	LH	Total	Inst.	HH	MH	LH	Total	Discrep.
III[13]	1	Fl2:6 Fl2:7 Cl:5 Hn:3 Tp:4 Tb:1	13	9	4	26	Pf1 Pf2		13	 6	19	Missing: 7HH, Poss: 4MH instead HH, 2LH instead HH
	2	Fl1:3 Fl2:4 Fl3:1 Tb:4 Db:3	8		7	15	Pf1 Pf2	8	 3		11	Missing:4LH, Poss: 3MH instead LH
	3	Fl1:7 Fl2:5 Fl3:4 Hn:1 Vc:7 Db:2	16		10	26	Pf1 Pf2	8 7	8		23	Missing: 1HH, 2MH, Poss: 8M instead LH
	4	Cl:1 Hn:2 Tp:7 Tb:3 Pf:17	17→	→ 8	→ 5	30	Pf1 Pf2	9	8 6	 5	28	Missing: 2HH
	5	Fl2:7 Fl3:3 Cl:8 Tp:3 Tb:2	10	11	2	23	Pf1 Pf2		13	 8	21	Missing: 2HH, Poss: 2MH instead HH, 6LH instead HH
	6	Fl1:1 Fl2:3 Fl3:7 Hn:5 Tp:4 Vc:8 Db:4	11	4	17	32	Pf1 Pf2	11	 11		22	Missing: 10LH, Poss: 7MH instead LH
	7	Fl1:5 Fl2:2 Cl:5 Hn:2 Tb:1 Vc:3 Db:7	7	5	13	25	Pf1 Pf2	9	2	 5	16	Missing: 1MH, 8LH, Poss: 2HH instead MH
	8	Fl2:1 Hn:3 Tp:2 Pf:24	24→ 1	→ 2	→ 3	30	Pf1 Pf2	12 3	12 3		30	Poss: 2HH instead LH, 1MH instead LH
	9	Fl1:4 FL2:5 Fl3:3 Tp:2 Vc:1	12	2	1	15	Pf1 Pf2	 7	8		15	Poss: 5MH instead HH, 1MH instead LH

Rehearsal nr.	Ictus	Inst.	HH	MH	LH	Total	Inst.	HH	MH	LH	Total	Discrep.
	10	Fl1:7 Fl3:8 Cl:5 Hn:4 Tb:3 Vc:6 Db:2	15	5	15	35	Pf1 Pf2	15		 7	22	Missing: 5MH, 8LH
IV[13]	11	Fl1:6 Fl2:11 Fl3:2 Cl:3 Tp:7 Vc:5	19	10	5	34	Pf1 Pf2		17 8		25	Missing: 4HH, 4LH, Poss: 15MH instead HH
	12	Fl1:6 Fl2:2 Hn:1 Tp:4 Tb:5 Db:3	8	4	9	21	Pf1 Pf2	12		 8	20	Missing: 1LH, Poss: 4HH instead MH
	13	Fl1:8 Fl2:1 Fl3:3 Cl:4 Hn:3 Tb:2 Vc:4	12	4	9	25	Pf1 Pf2	 9		10	19	Missing: 3HH, 3MH, Poss: 1LH instead MH
	14	Fl1:4 Fl2:1 Fl3:9 Tp:2 Tb:1 Vc:7 Db:2	14	2	10	26	Pf1 Pf2	15 2	 1	 7	25	Missing: 1MH(?), Poss: 3HH instead LH
	15	Cl:4 Hn:1 Tp:6 Tb:4 Db:6		10	11	21	Pf1 Pf2		10 10		20	Missing: 1LH, Poss: 10MH instead LH
	16	Fl1:1 Fl2:1 Fl3:9 Cl:4 Tp:1	11	5		16	Pf1 Pf2	10		 4	14	Missing: 1HH, 1MH, Poss: 4LH instead MH
	17	Fl1:3 Fl2:2 Fl3:1 Tb:3 Vc:2	6		5	11	Pf1 Pf2		6 5		11	Poss: 6MH instead HH, 5MH instead LH

Rehearsal nr.	Ictus	Inst.	HH	MH	LH	Total	Inst.	HH	MH	LH	Total	Discrep.
	18	Fl1:1 Fl2:2 Fl3:5 Hn:4 Tp:7 Vc:5 Db:1	8	7	10	25	Pf1 Pf2	10	 2	 6	18	Missing: 3MH, 4LH, Poss: 2HH instead MH
	19	Fl1:2 Fl2:3 Fl3:2 Hn:2 Tp:4 Tb:6	7	5	8	20	Pf1 Pf2	 9	8	6	23	Extra: 2HH, 1MH, Poss: 2MH instead LH
	20	Fl3:4 Cl:6 Hn:4 Tp:1 Tb:2 Vc:4 Db:3	4	7	13	24	Pf1 Pf2	9		5 5	19	Missing: 5LH, 1LH, Poss: 2HH instead MH, 2HH instead LH
V[13]	21	Fl1:5 Cl:6 Tb:3 Vc:1	5	6	4	15	Pf1 Pf2		 5	10	15	Poss: 5LH instead HH, 1LH instead MH
	22	Hn:4 Pf:24	24→	→	→ 4	28	Pf1 Pf2	 7	14 7		28	Poss: 4MH instead LH
	23	Fl1:8 Fl3:5 Cl:6 Hn:1 Tp:3 Vc:5 Db:4	13	9	10	32	Pf1 Pf2	 11		10	21	Missing: 2HH, 9MH
	24	Cl:7 Hn:4 Tb:2		7	6	13	Pf1 Pf2		 4	9	13	Poss: 3LH instead MH
	25	Fl1:7 Fl2:4 Fl3:2	13			13	Pf1 Pf2	13		 1	14	Extra: 1LH
	26	Fl1:4 Fl3:6 Cl:2 Hn:5	10	2	5	19	P1 P2		10	 7	17	Missing: 2 HH, Poss: 6 MH instead HH 2 LH instead HH
	27	Fl1:1 Fl2:6 Cl:7 Tp:4 Tb:3	7	11	3	21	P1 P2	 11		10	21	Poss: 4 HH instead MH, 7 MH instead LH

Rehearsal nr.	Ictus	Inst.	HH	MH	LH	Total	Inst.	HH	MH	LH	Total	Discrep.
	28	Fl1:5 Fl2:3 Fl3:4 Hn:5 Tp:4 Tb:7 Vc:6	12	4	18	34	P1 P2	5 8	3 6	7	29	Missing: 5 LH, Poss: 1 HH instead LH, 6 MH instead LH
	29	Fl1:3 Fl2:5 Fl3:3 Cl:1 Hn:3 Tp:2 Tb:4	11	3	7	21	P1 P2	11		 5	16	Missing: 3 MH, 2 LH
	30	Cl:4 Tb:6		4	6	10	P1 P2			6 5	11	Extra: 1LH, Poss: 4 LH instead MH
I[14]	31	Fl1:6 Fl2:8 Fl3:5 Hn:2 Tp:7 Vc:4	19	7	6	32	P1 P2	6 7	8 2	5 4	32	Poss: 3MH instead HH, 3LH instead HH
	32	Cl:5 Hn:6 Tb:4 Vc:9 Db:7		11	20	31	P1 P2		 10	12	22	Missing: 1MH, 8LH
	33	Tp:6 Pf:24	24	→ 6	→	30	P1 P2	 5	12		17	Missing: 13 LH(?)
	34	Fl1:4 Fl2:3 Fl3:6 Hn:5 Tp:2 Db:5	13	2	10	25	P1 P2	7		 5	12	Missing: 6 HH, 2 MH, 5 LH
	35	Fl1:3 Fl2:7 Fl3:2 Hn:4 Tp:1 Tb:1 Vc:6 Db:2	12	1	13	26	P1 P2		11	 8	19	Missing: 7HH, Poss: 4MH instead HH, 5MH instead LH

Rehearsal nr.	Ictus	Inst.	HH	MH	LH	Total	Inst.	HH	MH	LH	Total	Discrep.
	36	Fl2:1 Fl3:2 Cl:6 Hn:1 Tb:5 Db:3	3	6	9	18	P1 P2		7	11	18	Poss: 1MH instead HH, 2 LH instead HH
	37	Fl1:5 Fl2:2 Cl:1 Vc:6	7	1	6	14	P1 P2	6 7		1	14	Poss: 5 HH instead LH, 1 HH instead HH
	38	Fl1:5 Fl2:2 Fl3:3 Cl:1 Tb:2 Vc:2 Db:4	10	1	8	19	P1 P2		10	7	17	Missing: 1 LH, 1MH(?), Poss: 10 MH instead HH
	39	Fl1:7 Fl2:3 Fl3:8 Cl:3 Hn:1 Tp:2 Tb:3	18	5	4	27	P1 P2	7	3 11	6	27	Poss: 2 LH instead HH, 11 MH instead HH
	40	Tp:7		7		7	P2	7			7	Poss: 7 HH instead MH

Discrepancies Page 18:

0 icti none
25 icti with fewer numbers in 2-piano version
3 icti with fewer numbers in ensemble version
0 icti empty in 2-piano version, but not in ensemble version
32 icti with numbers shifted in range.

Rehearsal nr.	Ictus	Inst.	HH	MH	LH	Total	Inst.	HH	MH	LH	Total	Discrep.
II[14]	1	Fl2:4 Fl3:7 Hn:2 Tb:1 Vc:2 Db:5	11		10	21	P1 P2	 2	11 1	 2	16	Missing: 5 HH, Poss 4 MH instead HH, 8 MH instead LH
	2	Fl1:2 Fl2:6 Fl3:5 Cl:7 Hn:6 Vc:4	13	7	10	30	P1 P2		11	 7	18	Missing: 12 HH, Poss 1 MH instead HH, 3 MH instead LH
	3	Fl1:4 Fl3:3 Tp:6 Tb:5	7	6	5	18	P1 P2	 7	11		18	Poss: 5 MH instead LH
	4	Fl1:5 Fl2:4 Cl:5 Tp:2 Tb:4 Vc:6 Db:3	9	7	13	29	P1 P2		11	 11	22	Missing: 7 HH, Poss 2 MH instead HH, 2 MH instead LH
	5	Fl1:7 Fl2:8 Fl3:7 Cl:5 Hn:3 Tp:5 Db:2	22	10	5	37	P1 P2		11 7	 5	23	Missing: 14 HH, Poss 8 MH instead HH
	6	Fl1:6 Fl2:6 Cl:2 Hn:2 Tb:4 Db:1	12	2	7	21	P1 P2	12 4	 2	 3	21	Poss: 4 HH instead LH
	7	Fl1:8 Fl3:2 Cl:6 Tp:2 Tb:3 Vc:4	10	8	7	25	P1 P2	7	5	 10	22	Missing: 3 HH, Poss 3 LH instead MH
	8	Fl3:9 Hn:4 Tp:1 Tb:2 Vc:7 Db:6	9	1	18	28	P1 P2			10 6	16	Missing: 9 HH, 1 MH, 2 LH

Rehearsal nr.	Ictus	Inst.	HH	MH	LH	Total	Inst.	HH	MH	LH	Total	Discrep.
	9	Fl1:6 Fl2:5 Cl:3 Hn:5 Tp:6 Vc:3 Db:2	11	9	10	30	P1 P2	11 7		 6	24	Missing: 2 MH, 4 LH, Poss 7 HH instead MH
	10	Fl2:8 Cl:7 Tp:4 Tb:6 Db:5	8	11	11	30	P1 P2	6	6 4	 3	19	Missing: 2 HH, 1 MH, 8 LH
(III)[14*]	11	Hn:4 Pf:24	24	→	→ 4	28	P1 P2	8 9	7		24	Missing: 4 (LH, or HH)
	12	Fl3:8 Cl:7 Hn:2 Tp:1 Tb:3	8	8	5	21	P1 P2		 8	10	18	Missing: 3HH Poss 5LH instead HH
	13	Fl2:4 Fl:5 Cl:3 Hn:1 Tp:2 Tb:4 Vc:4 Db:2	9	5	11	25	P1 P2		11	 5	16	Missing: 9 HH, Poss 11MH instead LH
	14	Fl1:5 Fl2:7 Fl3:3 Cl:6 Hn:5 Tb:1 Vc:2 Db:1	15	6	9	30	P1 P2	 10		8	18	Missing: 5 HH, 6 MH, 1 LH
	15	Fl1:7 Fl2:9 Fl3:4 Hn:1 Tb:4 Vc:6 Db:4	20		15	35	P1 P2	8	8 10		24	Missing: 11 HH, Poss 1 MH instead HH, 15 MH instead LH
	16	Fl1:10 Fl3:7 Cl:5 Hn:4 Tp:2 Vc:3 Db:7	17	7	14	38	P1 P2	 10		12	22	Missing: 7 HH, 7 MH, 2 LH

Rehearsal nr.	Ictus	Inst.	HH	MH	LH	Total	Inst.	HH	MH	LH	Total	Discrep.
	17	Fl2:6 Cl:8 Tp:1 Tb:3 Vc:1	6	9	4	19	P1 P2		 8	10	18	Missing: 1 HH, Poss 5 LH instead HH, 1 LH instead MH
	18	Fl1:8 Fl3:7 Hn:2 Tp:1 Db:4	15	1	6	22	P1 P2	8 1	7 2		18	Missing:4 HH, Poss 2 MH instead HH, 6 MH instead LH
	19	Fl2:9 Fl3:2 Cl:3 Tp:4 Tb:1	11	5	1	17	P1 P2		11	 3	14	Missing: 3 HH, Poss 6 MH instead HH, 2 LH instead HH
	20	Fl1:5 Fl2:2 Fl3:4 Cl:1 Hn:3 Tp:8 Db:5	11	9	8	28	P1 P2	11		 6	17	Missing: 9 MH, 2 LH
(IV)[14*]	21	Fl1:11 Fl2:1 Fl3:9 Cl:4 Tb:2 Vc:8 Db:4	21	4	14	39	P1 P2	14	 6	 6	26	Missing: 7 HH, 2 MH, 8 LH
	22	Fl2:7 Fl3:1 Cl:2 Hn:5 Tp:4 Tb:6	8	6	11	25	P1 P2	14		 8	22	Missing: 3 LH, Poss 6 MH instead HH,
	23	Fl1:6 Fl2:12 Fl3:3 Cl:5 Hn:3 Tp:6 Tb:2 Db:5	21	11	10	42	P1 P2	14		 10	24	Missing: 7 HH, 11 MH

Rehearsal nr.	Ictus	Inst.	HH	MH	LH	Total	Inst.	HH	MH	LH	Total	Discrep.
	24	Fl1:9 Fl2:9 Fl3:15 Cl:8 Hn:5 Tp:7 Tb:4 Vc:3 Db:2	33	15	14	62	P1 P2	14		 10	24	Missing: 19 HH, 15 MH, 4 LH
	25	Fl1:12 Fl2:14 Fl3:19 Cl:11 Hn:8 Tp:11 Tb:7 Vc:12 Db:7	45	22	34	101	P1 P2	14 7	 6	9 5	41	Missing: 24 HH, 16 MH, 20 LH

*: Rehearsal number is incomplete, the Roman numeral is missing.

Discrepancies Page 19:

0 icti none
23 icti with fewer numbers in 2-piano version
0 icti with fewer numbers in ensemble version
15 icti with numbers shifted in range.

Discrepancies total:

155 icti none
243 icti with fewer numbers in 2-piano version
41 icti with fewer numbers in ensemble version
2 icti empty in 2-piano version, but not in ensemble version, or 3 if the extra ictus that only exists in the 2-piano version is counted as well
484 icti with numbers shifted in range.

NB:
HH: high high register
MH: middle high register
LH: low high register
HL: high low register
ML: middle low register
LL: low low register

The shift in range is not always certain, since some instruments could be seen as both MH and LH. But, as MF says all notes should be in the high register, I have taken this as a starting point, and decided that flutes are HH, clarinet and trumpet MH, horn and trombone LH, cellos and double basses LH, and the piano straddles all three ranges. For the section that is indicated to be low sounds only (in this analysis printed in red) the instruments were given the following ranges: flutes, clarinet and trumpet HL, horn, trombone and cellos ML, double basses LL and the piano again straddles all three ranges.

Ixion
Performance Issues

In this chapter I will discuss various problems and issues that arise when performing Ixion in either version. The nature of the score is such that some fundamental decisions need to be made on elements like choice of pitch, tone colour, rhythm and vibrato when the materials provided will not necessarily give unambiguous instructions. Comparing the two versions from a performance viewpoint has some extra problems when we compare the ensemble and the 2-piano version, as performers would need to decide if we are dealing with two totally independent pieces or one piece with an original scoring and a piano reduction.

Ensemble version

When faced with a score as open as *Ixion*, there are a number of very specific decisions that need to be made. The performance instructions are a mix of clarity and obscurity, with some elements being explained and others being left completely open or explained less than sufficiently. The full text of the instructions, printed in both versions of the score, is as follows:

IXION was commissioned by Merce Cunningham for his dance, "Summer Space." It is to be played in the high registers of the instruments except for a brief section in which the low registers are indicated.

Numbers indicate the amount of sounds to be played on or within the box, each box being equal to MM or thereabouts. The dynamics are low, with an occasional loud sound freely chosen by the performer.

If there are too many sounds for the wind or brass instruments to play, articulate as many as possible, and flutter or double-tongue the rest, avoiding glissando. If there are too many single sounds for the piano to play, the remaining sounds are simultaneous. All brass instruments and cellos with mutes. Cellos and basses should "mix" pizz and arco.

IXION is scored for cellos (3 to 7), basses (2 to 4), 3 flutes, clarinet, trumpet, horn, trombone, piano.

FIGURE 13

Morton Feldman, *Ixion*, preface (1958).

If we go through the text carefully, and apply the instructions to the ensemble version, the first thing we see (after being informed the piece was intended for a dance, which does not necessarily say a lot about the actual act of performance or interpretation), is the instruction that the whole piece, with the exception of one brief section, is to be played in the high registers of the instruments.[1]

This in itself is clear enough, even though it will mean that either each individual performer, or the conductor, will have to decide where on their instrument the high register starts.

In a lot of Feldman's graph pieces each instrument has a part divided in 3 layers, high, middle and low, so it is clear that the performer will need to take the entire range of the instrument and divide it into three parts. It is not stated if these divisions need to be of equal size, or need to be the same if there is more than one of a particular instrument. Each performer therefore will have to make up their own mind and take their own decisions, or the conductor would have to take an executive decision for everyone, although one can argue that this would go against the spirit of individual freedom of choice that characterises the graph pieces.

Furthermore, even though some instruments, like the piano, the harp, or the vibraphone (the last two are not used in *Ixion*), have a fixed range, most instruments have no clearly defined upper limit, being entirely dependent on the technical abilities of the individual performer. For the 2-piano version David Tudor took the upper half of the piano's range to work with, but then the instructions that were given to him are different from the ones in the printed score. The brief section mentioned before is the part between rehearsal numbers V^6 and III^7, where the score indicates 'low', meaning that every player (or the conductor) needs to make the same kind of decision on where their low register starts and ends.

Again, this is not always clear, in that string instruments and keyboards have a clearly defined bottom note, as do woodwinds, but the lowest note is less clear for brass instruments, where the use of pedal tones can extend the range downwards depending on the technical abilities of the player. Connected to this is the instruction "the dynamics are low, with an occasional loud sound freely chosen by the performer". For some instruments (strings, piano) any pitch can be played at any dynamic with the same kind of ease, but specifically for a lot of wind instruments this is definitely not the case. It is quite difficult to play very high notes on for example the flute, clarinet or horn very quietly, something that might conceivably have an impact on the decision on the boundaries of the range used. Performers can choose to leave the extreme high notes for those they will be playing loud, and keep the rest in a safer range, making it possible for them to give each note the same quiet dynamic. Alternatively, they might take the risk, and have notes that either do not speak and are therefore inaudible, or end up being louder than anticipated. For the loud sounds every performer will need to determine the meaning of 'occasional', as there is no specification provided. Would this be one in ten notes, one in a hundred, one every minute? It is left open as something to be decided on at the moment of performance, or possibly beforehand.

The second half of the third sentence is one that leaves us with a true conundrum. The first part is clear enough, stating that a number in a box indicates the amount of sounds to be played on or within the box. This means that each player can choose if a sound will be exactly on the beat, so to speak, or at any given moment within the duration of the box. Also, it is not specified how long a sound can be, so the sound can have a minimum duration of the shortest sound a performer can produce, and a maximum duration of the length of one box, or ictus. In ensemble performances this has sometimes led to a decision, most likely made by the conductor, that might be seen as valid in itself, but showing a limited interpretation of the instruction: a player can start a note anywhere during the length of the box, but they will have to keep the note going until the end of the length. This I feel would contradict the description Feldman gave of the piece as being 'pointillistic'. A case might be made for this interpretation of the length of individual sounds where we look at the instructions for other graph pieces such as *Intersection 3*, where the instructions say that "Sustained sounds once played must be held to the end of the notated duration." However, the preface for Ixion does not say anything about length of any kind and it would be safe to assume that rules in general would not be valid for any other piece than the one in whose preface they appear.

My interpretation of the score instructions is that Feldman is giving total freedom for the performer to give each sound any length as long as a sound starts anywhere within the duration of the box and does not exceed the length of the box. Where the number of sounds is greater than 1 the last sound played should not spill over into the next box, but there does not seem to be any need to fill up each box to the right, just as there is no need to fill a box from the left border.

Note that Feldman uses the word 'sound', not 'pitch', which strictly speaking could imply that performers are free to produce non-pitched sounds. However, this might be a very free interpretation of the rules. With only a few exceptions, generally because the instrumentation of the piece uses non-pitched percussion instruments [e.g. *Marginal Intersection* (1951), ...*Out of 'Last Pieces'* (1961)], Feldman's musical thinking, and as a result his use of instruments tends to be very much pitch oriented. Feldman, contrary to Cage, has never really been that interested in allowing all kinds of external sounds to enter his music, and he has not used extended techniques in any of his pieces, making it highly unlikely that he would have seen the word 'sounds' as anything else than meaning 'pitched sounds'. Still, if taken literally (more the letter of the law than the spirit of the law), one could make a case for having the freedom to include non-pitched sounds.

The second part of the sentence poses the real problem: "each box being equal to MM or thereabouts". As MM is used as an indication for tempo (being an abbreviation of Maelzel's Metronome or Metronome Mark), by giving the amount of beats per minute, it is problematic that in the instructions no number is given, making it impossible to know the desired tempo.

Since Feldman does give proper metronome marks for the vast majority of his works, and generally gives clear indications for the pieces that do not have one, this is either an oversight that never got corrected, or there is a good reason for not filling in a number after the MM.

It seems that the latter might be the case here.

If we look at the history of *Ixion* we see that Cunningham did not fix a precise duration for the dance and he advised that it would be "roughly 15 to 17 minutes long" and that "Mr. Feldman's score allows for this"[2]. Still, it does not give us a solution as to how to determine the tempo. If the length of the piece is given as being between 15 and 17 minutes, and we take the tempo within the piece itself as unchanging, then the MM needs to be between 43.82 and 49.66, roughly 44 to 50 beats per minute, a tempo range which does make the piece quite performable.

However, this does not seem to be the whole story.

In his book *The Graph Music of Morton Feldman*, David Cline describes a version of the score that seems to have been made by John Cage, who very probably conducted the first performances of *Ixion*. This version, done on paperboard, has a number of indications for tempo changes, entrances of specific dancers, and does not wholly correspond to the final published version of the score.[3] It is not clear if this version of the piece was done by Cage with or without Feldman's express consent, even though it is very likely that Feldman did not object, as one would expect some evidence of this. Also, in an interview with Joe Orton and Gavin Bryars dating from 1976 Feldman said:

> I didn't see the dance. I just asked Merce to tell me the time structure which I then decided to regulate in various ways, in other ways, and change the structures like oilcloth. If the dance was taking a little longer he would be a little slower. You know Cage's lecture on 'Indeterminacy'... so it's like an oilcloth but with plenty of material to work with, to either shorten or lengthen.[4]

This would give some license to be flexible with the score, at least when used with the dance, but whether it would also allow the same kind of flexibility when doing a concert performance of the piece might be a matter of some debate. The published score for both versions of *Ixion* does not explicitly give any kind of freedom in tempo other than not providing a metronome marking, and it would in my opinion be highly problematic to use an unpublished version of the score, made by someone else, as providing licence to be flexible in tempo. Still, the score does not contain any indication of a total duration, so one might speculate that the choice of tempo can be totally up to the performers.

There is an additional issue, as even though *Ixion* was initially composed for performance with dance, it can and does exist as a standalone piece, and can be performed in any kind of concert environment. It is not self-evident that the performance instructions for playing the piece with the dance should be identical to those needed without the dance. In a performance with dance it might be necessary to alter tempo to adapt to whatever is happening on stage, but this would not need to apply to a concert performance. The preface given mentions the dance but does not say anything specific about any flexibility needed in any situation, so the decision to be flexible with tempo would not be an obvious one at all.

The next instruction is more or less unproblematic: in the score Feldman uses numbers ranging from 0 (where the box is left empty instead of having the number 0 in it) to 24, which indicates that a player needs to fit 24 sounds into the time space of one ictus.

Even in the slower tempo of 44 boxes per minute, the performer has to fit 24 sounds into 1.36 seconds. It is true that the piano is the only instrument with 24 sounds in one box, and due to the nature of the instrument it is a lot easier to fit this amount of material in the prescribed time, as Feldman allows for simultaneous sounds to happen:

If there are too many single sounds for the piano to play, the remaining sounds are simultaneous.[5]

This instruction makes it clear that in principle, a number given in a box indicates the number of separate attacks, and that Feldman considers a chord as a simultaneous occurrence of multiple sounds. A sound, therefore, should be seen as a single pitch, whether the instrument is capable of producing chords or not, a notion that would be important for the pianist and the string players. The highest number occurring in the other parts is 19 (the last box of the piece in flute III), which is very probably more than any but the most virtuosic players would be able to fit in 1.36 seconds.

In this, and other cases where the number is too high to be performed as separate pitches, Feldman gives the freedom, but only for the wind and brass instruments, to:

> articulate as many as possible, and flutter or double-tongue the rest, avoiding glissando.[6]

Just as with the piano part, adherence to this rule would mean that each player will need to determine from box to box how many of the prescribed number of sounds they can play as separate attacks, get these in first, and end the box with either a chord or chords (piano), or a flutter or double tongue (winds and brass). The result will necessarily be that boxes would tend to be fuller at the end than at the beginning. Whether this is actually audible, given that, if we stick to the time length of 15 to 17 minutes for the whole piece, a box will have a length of between 1.2 and 1.36 seconds, is open to discussion, and the theoretical density of these over-full boxes could be considered a moot point. It is interesting to see that there is no provision for the strings for fitting in large numbers of sounds. This might be because the highest number appearing in the cello part is 12 (only occurring once, in the very last box), and the rest of the piece does not go above 9, and the double bass part never goes about 7, making it quite possible to fill each box with the required number of separate single sounds. The indication to use flutter of double tongueing also implies that pitch repetition is allowed so it is not necessary to alter the pitch with each sound articulated.

All brass instruments and all cellos are instructed to play with mute. Feldman does not prescribe any particular kind of mute – and especially for trumpet and trombone there is a large collection to choose from – so the exact sound quality is open to the individual player's choice. Brass players might even opt for more than one mute and change during the piece; there is no instruction that would make this impossible or undesirable. It is curious that the double basses are not instructed to use mutes, even though these do exist, and definitely existed at the time of composing *Ixion* in 1958. It is not known why Feldman made this particular decision. We do see that in the score of *The Straits of Magellan*, he prescribes mutes for the horn and trumpet, but not for the double bass. In *Atlantis* again the cello and brass are with sordino throughout, but the double bass has no such indication. However, here the double bass instruction is 'Pizz. throughout', which could explain why Feldman might feel there would be no need for a mute. The cello is also pizzicato, except for bowed harmonics, so the use of a mute would therefore be justified. In fact, having looked at as many of Feldman's orchestral scores, it seems that prescribing mutes for the double basses is very much an exception, with, as far as I could find, only the 1972 piece, *Cello and Orchestra* having this instruction in the score. One wonders if this might actually have been an error rather than a conscious choice.

Going back to *Ixion*, the cellos and basses are instructed to "mix" pizzicato and arco, and both implementation and ratio is left completely free for each player. The final sentence in the instructions gives the scoring of the piece. In itself quite clear, but it does raise a performance issue: the score calls for 3 to 7 cellos and 2 to 4 basses. However, contrary to the 3 flute players, who each have their own distinctive part, there is only one part for cellos, and one for the basses, implying that all the cello players play the same part, as do the bass players, which is in line with traditional orchestral practice. Due to the nature of the parts, where each player is free to determine both pitch, exact moment of entrance, and length of each sound, it would necessarily result in the number for each box in the cello and bass parts being multiplied by the number of players, making the total number of sounds in each performance dependent on the number of string players. It would be not only impractical, but actually going against the idea of the notation, to fix the parts in advance so that all cellos, and all basses would play the same sounds. It is interesting to see that in this respect Feldman thought of the score as orchestral, rather than chamber music, as in the majority of orchestral scores all wind players would have their own individual part, but the string players would not, and there would be one part per string part, independent of the number of players. In chamber music the number of individual parts is usually identical to the number of performers, so *Ixion* in this respect is thought of as a piece for chamber orchestra.

I have already mentioned the use of the word 'sounds' and its possible implication of giving license to use unpitched sounds as well as pitches, but there is another important issue that needs an informed decision from the performers. This pertains to the exact nature of pitches used. As Feldman does not want to prescribe anything but the basic information on register, the musicians have to give a lot of thought about what kind of pitch material they want to use for the piece. This is closely linked to the idea of idiom, style, and period, but the matter is not at all straightforward. As Feldman says nothing at all about the nature of the pitch (sound) material to be chosen, each performer is in principle free to make their own decisions, opening up the way to avenues of thinking that would be, again, correct if one only looks at the letter of the law, but are very problematic with regards to the spirit. One could easily decide, because it is the kind of material one prefers to play, to make a completely tonal version of the part, and only to use pitches that fit into standard tonal harmonic rules. There is no provision in the instructions to counter this. Or, one could make a non-chromatic version, that is to say, include intervals smaller than a minor second, and make a microtonal version. Again, this would not be against the rules given. As long as players adhere to the general high (or low) register, any pitch chosen would be acceptable in theory. In practice, these decisions would go against Feldman's idea of the sound of the work. To understand this, we have to look at the specific performance practice of Feldman's works in the 1950's and the general performance attitudes of the time.

From the earlier part of the 20th century, contemporary music performance had developed into something that was deemed more and more for specialised performers. The relationship between composers and musicians seemed to be evermore disconnected, and the amount of contemporary music programmed at non-specialised concert series had shrunk dramatically. Describing the reasons for this would go beyond the scope of this text, but in brief, it was generally felt that a lot of composers had lost contact with the audience, or the audience had lost contact with the composers. Even though this is nothing new, and pieces belonging to the avant-garde of their day were mostly greeted with puzzlement, disdain, or outright hostility, concert programming throughout the

19th century usually included at least some recently composed pieces.

By 1950 this practice had all but died out, and contemporary music, especially those works considered to belong to the avant-garde, had retreated into their own small circle. Composers would generally write for a few dedicated musicians, performers who knew exactly what was expected from them, who were happy to work closely with the composer to make sure the work was given a rendition that came closest to what was needed. This is similar to how composers worked throughout the centuries, and there is nothing exceptional in writing for either yourself, as Feldman did as well, or for your close allies; the main change is that public performances would have retreated mostly to intimate spaces, often not primarily meant for music performances, such as art galleries and people's homes.

It could be said that avant-garde music making is reminiscent of the small gatherings that composers like Franz Schubert would have to premiere their compositions in the 1820s. The circle around Feldman was quite small, and consisted chiefly of the pianist David Tudor, Feldman himself, John Cage (as pianist and conductor), as well as cellist Seymour Barab – who very probably gave the first performance of Feldman's first graph piece *Projection 1*, and violinist Frances Magnes, who is the dedicatee of *Projection 4*.

Pieces were generally composed with these musicians in mind, and there was a close collaboration on every aspect of the performance. This meant that not only could Feldman be sure that the works would be performed according to his wishes, the performers would be well versed in Feldman's compositional idiom and musical language. Problems would often arise when pieces were performed by larger groups that were not specialised in playing new music, being worst when working with orchestras. The attitudes of a substantial part of orchestral players were quite hostile to avant-garde pieces and the non-standard demands they would make. There are numerous stories of performances being totally sabotaged by players either not taking anything in the piece seriously or trying their best to subvert the rules of a particular composition as much as possible. John Cage described a performance of his *Atlas Eclipticalis* with *Winter Music* by the New York Philharmonic Orchestra conducted by Leonard Bernstein in 1964 as 'criminal':

> The seventy or so Philharmonic instrumentalists, their contact microphones attached to a bank of amplifiers, were supposed to play through Cage's piece for eight minutes. Instead, many of them improvised freely, ran through scales, quoted other works, talked, fooled with the electronic devices, or simply sat on the stage without playing. "They acted criminally," Cage said, some even stomping on their microphones. Christian Wolff was present and thought the musicians "shocking, really, really awful. ... They deliberately sabotaged; they killed the piece. Literally, I mean, before your very eyes on the stage.[7]

Jorge Mester, who conducted the orchestra for a performance of *Ixion* at the New York State Theatre in 1965, recalls:

> It was an unfortunate but sadly hilarious occasion. I dutifully rehearsed the orchestra as best I could, making sure they understood Feldman's instructions. We then proceeded to the pit for the dress (and only) run-through. About eight minutes into the dance, one of the dancers

> leapt from the wings, whereupon the trumpet player tooted a tune from "The Grand Canyon Suite [by Ferde Grofé] – the orchestra fell apart with mirth and was unable to continue.[8]

Feldman himself recalls another instance where orchestra players clearly sabotaged a piece:

> I would designate a certain amount of notes to play in the graph things, and I would hear 'Yankee Doodle' coming out of the horn section. The players decide together, before the concert, actually to sabotage it – and they decided in this particular section they were going to play 'Yankee Doodle', with the amount of notes called for and in the register of the score.[9]

These would have been quite extreme situations and would not form the majority of performance experiences with musicians from further afield than the inner circle of performers, but even when the players would be trying to follow the instructions to the letter, it would not always mean that the result was to Feldman's liking. Feldman describes one example of this in an interview with Dore Ashton:

> Unfortunately, one of the situations that happened [...] is that we began to hear the instrumentalists making my particular composition. The reason that was happening is because even though in my own mind I was hearing sound very abstractly, every time – for example, one particular piece [10] where it's most obvious – every time the xylophone would have, say, four seconds for a solo situation in which, even though I would give him the amount of sounds to

> play in that particular situation, even though I would tell him how to play it, what he actually played was of such a horrendous nature that I realized that there was something wrong.[11]

This presents the potential performer with a clear indication that, even though Feldman instructs the player to freely choose any sounds they want, it isn't that simple, as there seems to be an unwritten requirement that the pitches chosen should be in line with the composer's preference.[12] As a performer you can take several different attitudes, depending on your personal idea about interpretation and freedom. Just looking at the score, without any external source material to draw upon, any pitch, or even any unpitched sound would do equally well, as long as they are high-sounding where indicated, and low-sounding where indicated.

This line of thinking would infer that a score should contain all the necessary information to make a performance according to the composer's wishes possible. Even though this is a performance philosophy that gained a lot of traction in the 20th century, and quite a few composers would maintain that performers only need to follow the score, and certainly not insert their own interpretation, it is clearly not the correct course of action here.

It is evident from looking at the score of *Ixion* that a lot of decisions are to be made by the performer; not just the sounds, but also the exact placement, and the exact duration within the boxes. Therefore, some level of interpretation is definitely needed, leading us to the question of how large this level of interpretation should be? In other words, does the performer still have a responsibility towards the composer that informs the choice of sounds, or do they have license to make the sounds completely their own?[12]

It turns out that, even though they are very often bunched together as composers who thought the same about composing and the role of the performer, Feldman's ideas about freedom were very different from those of John Cage. Cage wanted to free himself, and the performers, from their own 'likes and dislikes', and was not interested in choosing one particular sound over another:

> [...] one may give up the desire to control sounds, clear his mind of music, and set about discovering means to let sounds be themselves rather than vehicles for man-made theories or expressions of human sentiments.[13]

Feldman never followed this line of thought, as he was too much preoccupied with the beauty of sounds and pitches, and not at all with allowing performers to do whatever they wanted. As we saw in Chapter 2, Ixion – history and scores, Feldman's thoughts and ideas behind his graph scores and their innate freedom came from a totally different mind-set. If a performer would choose to take this mind-set to influence their decision-making when performing *Ixion*, or any of the other graph pieces, this would automatically imply that some thorough research is needed into the specific sound world of Feldman's music at that time. One way of doing this would be by looking at scores written in the same period (rather than pieces written later in his compositional output, that might have a different harmonic language) – and in the case of *Ixion* these would include pieces such as *Two Pieces for Six Instruments*, *Three Pieces for String Quartet*, *Two Pianos*, and *Last Pieces* for piano, all of which give a good idea of the harmonies and pitch distributions that Feldman was interested in at that time.

This knowledge would then potentially influence the choice of sounds when performing *Ixion*. It does presuppose a willingness of the performer to engage fully with the idiom of the piece at hand, something that is generally found very prevalent with chamber music performers, but not necessarily with orchestral players, mainly due to the very different pressures of time and size of repertoire they have to deal with. There is often simply not enough time to familiarise oneself with the exact demands of music that is wholly unlike any other music that makes up the vast bulk of the repertoire, and orchestral players understandably rely on conductors to give them all the information they need.

In the case of sabotage and hostility, which do seem to be one-off incidents rather than regular occurrences, an investigation into the exact causes would venture more into the realms of music psychology and anthropology and would therefore fall outside of the scope of this book. As Feldman's pieces were mostly performed by either himself or musicians very close to him, there was no need to be more specific, and all performers involved knew exactly what sounds would be needed to make the piece fit its creator's musical wishes or expectations. As John Cage remarked "Morty's notated music is Morty playing his graph music"[14], implying that the exact nature of sound that he wanted for his graph music was no different than that of his non-graph pieces, and that therefore the freedom given to the performer was not absolute, but an invitation to choose freely within the appropriate musical language. Feldman admitted "And that was the big problem I had"[15]. In an interview with British composer Howard Skempton from 1977, Feldman makes some additional remarks on musicians' attitudes towards pitch and rhythmical choices, which would eventually lead him away from graph notation, and back to conventionally notated scores:

> HS: […] Possibly in the graph pieces people would do things which would distract from what you were trying to do. You were trying to create a weight, and they would play a major third, or a triad. You would say that's not a weight of three notes, that's a triad. So, this is probably what led you to fully notate works.
>
> MF: I found that – and Cage talks about this now himself continuously – people mistake freedom for license. And I feel that there's a problem. There's also a problem in terms of the conventional training of musicians. […] Certain instruments had to prepare passages because the whole make-up of the instrument, in a sense, is diatonic. Like the harp. You know, I'd never adopted a pitch structure, how to get my pitches. But I hear them. I hear them like this! [snaps fingers] No problem! I hear and I write down the pitches. There's no problem! It's just nothing! So I decided to do it myself. Also there was a problem where everybody was very metric-oriented. […] That they were only interested, and still are only interested, that if they see a note on the beat, it's a note on the beat. And everything people cannot understand, say the difference between breathing a sound and its metric unit.[16]

These remarks bring us to the other major issue performers will need to make decisions on: rhythm, and placement of sounds in time. The preface of *Ixion* states that sounds can be played on or within the box, implying that the box is only a container that will hold a number of sounds, but does not prescribe the exact placement of these sounds within the box. Sounds can start anywhere within the duration, and can last a maximum of one unit, but within the box, can be any length, ideally resulting in an extremely free-flowing rhythmical structure, where any real sense of a beat is not present. Every individual performer can of course choose to articulate the start of each box, but it would be against Feldman's and the music's intentions to have one person (in all probability the conductor) to determine this for all players. Still, in at least one performance of the ensemble version of *Ixion* exactly this decision seems to have been made in a specific part of the score, namely the part between one ictus before III^{12} and 8 after II^{13}, where most of the boxes contain the number 1 for all players. In the recording by the Eos Ensemble, conducted by Jonathan Scheffer, in this passage all boxes containing 1 are played at the start of the ictus (on the beat), so suddenly there is a 45-second passage where the rhythmical identity of the piece is completely different and uniform. It is debatable, even though it is not violating anything stated in the preface, whether it would be an appropriate decision. It might have been a conscious choice to make these pages sounds as much as possible as they look, but it does sound very much like a *Fremdkörper*.[17] (Fig. 14)

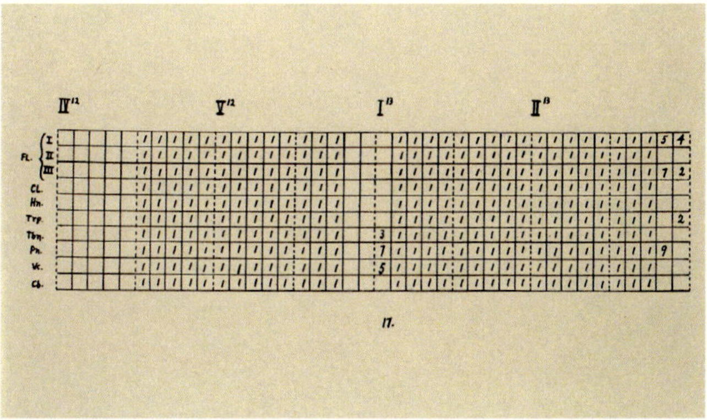

FIGURE 14

Morton Feldman, *Ixion*, ensemble version, page 17 (1958).

In addition, if we look at the same passage in the 2-piano version we see that this will never be a possible outcome, as the boxes are not all filled with the same number (Fig. 15):

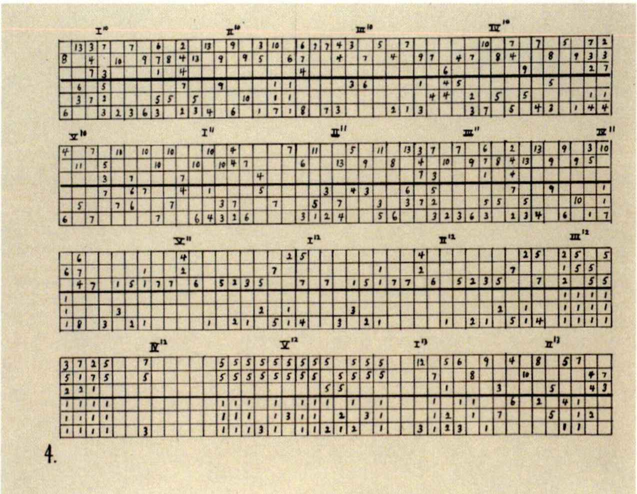

FIGURE 15

Morton Feldman, *Ixion*, 2-piano version, page 4 (1958).

One other aspect that would need to be considered, is the overall sound world of the piece itself. The piece was meant to be a kind of aural equivalent to Rauschenberg's set and costume design, which were described as 'pointillistic'. I would say that this term was not just used to echo the school of painting developed in France in the 1880s by Georges Seurat and Paul Signac, wherein an image was built up out of numerous small dots and strokes of paint, making the separate colours blend in the viewer's eye into a larger overall subdued and pastel-like field. As Rauschenberg was more interested in the idea that the dancers would disappear into the set when not moving and create a strong shimmering when in motion, where the dots on the costumes interacted with the similarly coloured dots on the set pieces, creating an almost moiré effect on the viewer's eyes.

Feldman's score would need to be seen as a combination of this and the idea of a musical pointillism, in which single, seemingly unrelated pitches would create clouds of sound with a constantly varying density, similar to painterly pointillism, but purely abstract.

All this would imply to me that the piece would be focused more on shorter sounds than longer ones and this makes the case for filling up every box from beginning to end, no matter how many sounds would need to be played, not necessarily the right musical and aesthetic choice.

To help the performers get to grips with unfamiliarity of the notation, combined with the customary lack of time for preparation in rehearsal, Cage came up with a solution for the first performance:

> Oh there've been so many problems. Remember that interesting one with, again, that piece of yours that Merce

> Cunningham used, "Ixion", where it was written on graph and used numbers and that was the piece, of course, and that was the way to read it. But through the exigencies of rehearsals and so forth, I translated it into something conventional – with quarter notes, you remember? – which was not what the piece was, but which permitted the musicians to quickly play it. Where the numbers meant that they would have had to devote themselves in a way that they actually didn't have the time or inclination to do.[18]

Determining what might be the best solution for choosing pitches and rhythm is of course very important for shaping the musical content of *Ixion*, but I would say just as important is the aesthetics of what kind of aural quality the sounds themselves would need to have.

To address this as a performer it would seem to be just as necessary to learn about the general performance practice of Feldman's work as it would be for any other piece of music. When performing Beethoven's music for instance, any musician who takes themselves seriously would need to familiarise themselves with the specific sound world of the composer and find the right kind of sound on their instrument. This is at least of equal importance for the very specific kind of sound world that Feldman's music inhabits and a thorough and deep involvement with this is of the utmost importance. Feldman's work from very early on has been mainly concerned with an exploration of low dynamics, where the vast majority of his compositions until the late 1960s would mention that dynamics need to be 'extremely low', 'very low', 'as soft as possible', or 'barely audible'. In some pieces he would put in traditional dynamic markings, but only in those few works that would have a broader dynamic range, such as the *3 Songs to e e cummings*, where the range goes from *pppp* to *f* (for two notes in the first song). Later on, the standard dynamic would be *ppp* with occasionally *ppppp* for some sections. This forces the performer to think very carefully about the nature of quietness in performing.

What, if we look at those works that have a general indication without the standard dynamic signs, would be meant by 'as soft as possible', let alone 'barely audible'? For whom is this intended, for the performer or the listener? The importance of this decision should not be underestimated.

I have been at performances of Feldman's works where the chosen dynamic was so low that no audience member sitting further back than row two could hear anything at all. Even though this is clearly following 'as soft as possible' to the letter, it does not necessarily make for a good performance when the performer is the only person able to hear the details of the score. I think it is very important here to always keep in mind the remark Feldman got from a chance meeting with Edgard Varèse on the streets of New York, where a very young Feldman was told to:

Think about the time it speaks from the stage to out there.[19]

This, by extension, is also valid for the dynamic of the sound travelling from the podium to the audience and would need to be adapted for each acoustical environment, where 'extremely quiet' is never an absolute value; some spaces are louder than others and the dynamic performed should be the one perceived rather than played.

A more problematic element of performance practice lies in the nature of the sound produced, that is, the colour, the core or heart of the sound itself. Even in low dynamics any note played on any instrument can have a large number of characteristics, from a gentle, mild sound to one with a sharp edge to it and anything in between. This can have to do with the nature of attack given to a note – although quite a few of Feldman's scores stipulate 'a minimum of attack' – or with the specific technique used by the performer in bowing or blowing. There are remarks Feldman made on occasion that can help us understand more about the kind of sound he expected from the musicians.

In one lecture Feldman reminisced on a performance of *Cello and Orchestra* where the cellist was asked to bring a different cello next time because Feldman felt the sound was too Piatigorsky-like, whereas he wanted something more Fournier-like. [20] [21]

Feldman also remarked on growing up hearing Heifetz,[22] which had a lasting influence on his thinking about sound quality. Feldman had piano lessons with Vera Maurina-Press, who studied with Ferruccio Busoni and was close friends with composer Alexander Scriabin. From Maurina-Press he inherited a particular attention to a specific tone quality which he described in the 1984 lecture in Darmstadt:

If you have a feeling, a tactile feeling for the instrument, and if you, just with your finger... [plays a couple of notes on the piano with one finger]. That I learned from my teacher. The way she would put her finger down, in the Russian way, just the finger, the lightness of the finger, and produce a B-flat... you wanted to faint! [23]

Those who have witnessed Feldman play the piano would often remark on his specific sound, made by simply laying his finger on the key and letting the weight of his hand do the rest, making for a tone that was soft and with almost no discernible attack. As a base from which a musician could start finding their own particular tone quality suitable for

Feldman's music this could be helpful. There are recordings available online of Fournier and Heifetz playing, and even when these are perhaps not ideal with regards to recording quality, they give a very good impression of the kind of tone production that was in Feldman's mind.

There are precious few recordings of Feldman himself playing, and the only ones that have any kind of online presence is a performance of *Why Patterns?* with Eberhard Blum on flutes and Jan Williams on Glockenspiel, [24] *Five Pianos* with Harrison Birtwistle, Stephen Savage, Roger Smalley and John Tilbury, [25] *Two pieces for three pianos* with Robert Moran and Loren Rush, [26] and *Piano Three Hands, Two Pianos* and *Vertical Thoughts 1* with Ingrid Lindgren. [27] Even so, as most of the piano music Feldman wrote in the 1950s and 1960s was specifically composed with David Tudor in mind, listening to these early recordings would be a perfect way into developing the sound one might want to aim for. The ensemble version of *Ixion* does state that there can be an occasional loud sound, but as the overall dynamic is low, I would feel it is justified to start any research into tone production here.

One thorny issue that admittedly would be of some limited importance to *Ixion* is that of the use of vibrato in string and wind instruments. If we take Feldman's remarks on Heifetz and Fournier to the letter, we could think that this would extend to their specific use of vibrato. However, performers will need to think very carefully if Feldman's music needs vibrato at all, at least in the graph pieces. Feldman did not remark on this often, if at all in his lectures and writings, and the only personal experience I have is of him liking the pure non-vibrato sound the Xenakis Ensemble produced when they performed *Trio* and *Piano, violin, viola, cello* in Middelburg in 1985 and 1987. In some later pieces such as *For John Cage*, Feldman actually indicates vibrato by using a specific notational device. The violin is asked to perform a tremolo on one bow between two enharmonically identical pitches (C-flat and A-double sharp on page 16 and D-double sharp and E natural on page 17 of the manuscript score). [28] When I asked Feldman about this he confirmed that this would result in a slight vibrato. As *Ixion* consists mostly of short sounds where the idea of vibrato is mostly irrelevant, as there is simply no time to implement this technique for most of the piece, and therefore the issue might not be of much importance. Even so, performers will need to decide when they choose to play a longer sound whether or not vibrato is felt to be appropriate. My personal view is that it is not.

I have already touched upon the role of the conductor but I think there is a need to say a bit more on this.

The piece clearly needs someone to make sure the ensemble stays coordinated but otherwise one could argue that the function of the conductor in *Ixion*, as it would be in other larger graph pieces, needs some special consideration. As within the piece sounds are mostly left to the individual performer's choice, this makes a conductor's role quite complicated and ambiguous.

How far should the conductor act as musical interpreter? Would the conductor need to make sure all performers are on the same page with regards to the kinds of decisions they make on what kinds of pitches are chosen, how many loud notes should be played, where sounds should be articulated within the boxes, what colour the strings would need to aim for?

It could be said that all these decisions need to be left to the individual players, but there is a risk of the piece sounding too disparate in sound production. The element of the piece that the conductor will definitely need to assert control over is tempo, and as we saw earlier, it seems that for the performances with Cunningham's choreography the tempo was not constant during the piece, even though the score does not say anything about this. Whether this means that in a concert performance the same flexibility needs to be present is not self-evident and one can argue that without specific instructions there is no need for anything but a strictly maintained tempo from beginning to end. Still, a conductor would need to think carefully about this and make an executive decision. All other performance elements could be influenced by the conductor or even prescribed, and this might be useful if it becomes clear that the individual players are too far apart in their own thinking to make the piece sound well balanced. Any conductor would need to make a personal decision on how much they would want to interfere with elements that are well within the individual performer's remit, such as the use of pizzicato and arco in the strings, flutter and tremolo, and chords when the density of the part makes the use of these features necessary, and perhaps the amount of loud sounds performers would play. I would say the conductor would want to have more of the role of an overseer than controller, and only interfere when things threaten to be unbalanced or when players do not follow the rules set out by the composer. In addition, they might want to make sure the overall rhythmic, intervallic and harmonic language is consistent and in line with what is seen as appropriate. For some of the more specialised ensembles, such as the Netherlands-based Ives Ensemble, a consensus is reached between players during the rehearsal process. Then again, the Ives Ensemble is used to working without a conductor, and is perhaps something of an outlier, as most groups focusing on contemporary music repertoire include a conductor, who assumes the same function as a conductor would have in front of a standard symphony orchestra, i.e. the conductor who makes most of the interpretative decisions and communicates these to the players.

2-piano version

A lot of the issues discussed above would be similar for the 2-piano version of *Ixion*, but there are, due to the nature of the instrumentation, some important differences. The fact that the score of the 2-piano version is preceded by the instructions for the ensemble version, means that some elements of this preface will not apply when performed by a piano duo, and that some elements are not explained at all.

First of all, the structure of the score is different, with three layers of boxes for each piano instead of just one for each instrument in the ensemble version. I have outlined these problems earlier in this chapter, such as what to decide for boundaries of range – all sounds are in the high register, but with three layers there might need to be a differentiation (and the same goes for the short passage in low register) between high high, middle high, and low high sounds.

This division is not explicit in the score, and therefore it is entirely feasible to think of all layers as simply 'high register', even if one takes the 2-piano version as being independent from the ensemble version, i.e. not a piano reduction, so that any rules and boundaries would not need to be transferred from one version to the other. Also, there is still the possibility to include non-pitched sounds, but, due to the nature of the piano, a microtonal version would be impossible without serious retuning of the instruments, something that would be a major practical, artistic, and aesthetic decision on the part of the performers, and not one likely to be made.

As for the 1-filled passage discussed above (one ictus before III[12] and 8 after II[13]) the 2-piano version does not have this feature, even though for some of this passage one of the pianos has a 1 in each of its boxes. Still, due to the fact that the three rows of boxes are performed by one player, chances of this being played in a completely regular way would be minimal.

Feldman provided Tudor with a handwritten set of explanatory notes dated 15 January 1960, [29] in which at least a few issues are made clear:

- Divide the top 4 octaves of the piano range (middle c to the highest c) into high, middle and low. For ↓ divide below middle c
- Entrance on or within the duration of beat
- Dynamics are free
- As many single notes as possible [30]

This set of instructions is unfortunately not printed in the published score of *Ixion*, 2-piano version, and it is therefore evident that potential performers would probably not be aware of them.

An important issue that would not arise in the ensemble version but does need serious thought in the 2-piano version is coordination. Where the ensemble would in all likelihood be led by a conductor, so that all icti would be clearly defined, having only two pianos would not warrant the use of a conductor, so other strategies have to be put in place.

In most music there is enough sense of a pulse for this not to be much of a problem, but in *Ixion* the pulse is not, or need not be, articulated. Also, because of the constantly changing nature of the piece, where from one rehearsal and/or performance to the next, pitches would be totally different, provided that the players do not use a previously fixed version of the score (see further below), performers cannot rely on audible cues.

Possible solutions for dealing with this problem include using a visual metronome, although synchronising these would potentially be quite tricky. There are ways of using one device shared by both players such as a flashing light that is placed in such a way that is visible to each pianist. This would, however, potentially be quite distracting for the audience and a more subtle way of making sure there is a shared light pulse would be necessary, using an aural click track, or having one of the performers give a clear visual pulse, usually done by nodding, though this might impede this performer's freedom more than would be seen as desirable, not to mention the physical distraction it could cause for the pianist giving these cues.

The psychology of performance makes it more than likely that the need for this regular physical movement will influence the rhythmic identity of the interpretation and make it less free and more bound to the pulse. If the 2-piano version is seen merely as a piano reduction for use during rehearsals only this problem would most likely not arise, as there would be a conductor present. However, as *Ixion* has been performed with the dance in both versions, it would be logical to assume a conductor would not necessarily have been involved other than with the ensemble version. Furthermore, having a rigidly fixed aural or visual click track has the additional drawback of functioning as a kind of musical straightjacket, which could seriously hamper the sense of flexibility and freedom that is integral to a musically valid performance of the piece. As we saw, the tempo could be somewhat flexible from one section to the next and making one single click track cannot take into account the fact that a vital part of any performance needs to react to the acoustical circumstances. The acoustics of the venue should, for any music, inform the musicians. A dry acoustic space could stand a somewhat faster pace than a very reverberant room. Another solution for coordinating the two parts, but one that would be potentially against the nature of the composition, is to prepare a specific, written-out score, that could be rehearsed as any conventionally notated piece.

David Tudor, however, did exactly this with *Intersection 2* and *Intersection 3*, so there is a precedent, but it could take away the spontaneity of having to choose the exact pitches at the moment of performance. In addition, the scores of both *Intersections* are extremely dense and the idea of performing these pieces without some predetermined strategy would most likely be impossible for most, perhaps all pianists.

Tudor actually prepared a written-out score of *Ixion*'s 2-piano version, but it is incomplete, and only has one of the piano parts. It is interesting to note that Tudor seems to go against at least one of Feldman's instructions for *Ixion*, which is that the piano should play as many single notes as possible, implying, just as it says in the preface for the ensemble version, that simultaneous sounds (i.e. chords) occur only when there is not enough time to play all required sounds as separate attacks. Tudor seems to focus quite a lot on playing chords, which would be more in line with the instructions for *Intersection 2* and *3*, where it merely says: "The numbers indicate how many keys one plays"[31], leaving the performer free to combine as many as needed or desired into aggregates.[32] The path Tudor and Cage chose, when they made a recording of the 2-piano version of *Ixion*, seems to have been not entirely in line with the pointillistic sound world Feldman had in mind, that was intended to be an aural equivalent to Rauschenberg's set and costumes.

The performance instructions do hand a lot of freedom to the performer in that it is not given how many separate notes will be played and how many are combined into chords and the ratio of single pitches to aggregates will naturally be different from one performer to the next, depending on the technical capabilities of each individual pianist and perhaps also on their personal aesthetic choices. The latter, if we take Feldman's performance instructions to the letter (and this would be valid for both the printed instructions and the unpublished rules that were given to Tudor), would need to play a minor role at best, as these clearly state the chords only come into play if the performer is not able to play the required number of notes as single pitches.

Still, a case can be made for some flexibility in thought and interpretation. It might be possible to play all the notes asked for as single notes but only in a kind of mad scramble and a more or less continuous state of panic, due to quite a few of the boxes having relatively high numbers. The decision for the performer would need to consider therefore the character and stylistic identity of the piece, something that is not only not apparent from the score, but is not mentioned in the performance instructions either, and would imply some amount of research into Feldman's sound world and musical language.

Even so, *Ixion* is somewhat of an outlier in Feldman's compositional output due to the overall density of the score, which is really only somewhat comparable to the earlier *Intersection 2* and *3* for piano, although the *Ixion* does not have the character of "a music like violently boiling water in some monstrous kettle" as Feldman wrote to Tudor in a letter dated 15 June 1953, referring to *Intersection 3*.

As mentioned above, *Ixion*'s sound world is thought of as a pointillist one, and this would have additional implications for the 2-piano version, especially when considering the use of the right or sustain pedal. There is no indication of any pedal use in the score at all, but the absence of something does not necessarily mean the absence of the thing itself, and to assume the piece should be played without any use of the sustain pedal would be wrong.

However, there are clear implications in using the pedal, both in overall sound and in the fact that it will prolong notes. Given that the instructions do not allow any sound to be held longer than the length of one box, the sustain pedal, if used, should only last for a maximum of one single box.

In addition, the nature of the piece would favour shorter durations over longer ones, implying a very sparse use of the pedal. The use of the left pedal, which in the vast majority of Feldman's compositions would be held continuously over the whole duration of the piece, analogous to the use of mutes for strings and brass instruments, could and should be left to the performers' discretion, as *Ixion* has a different dynamic range than most pieces. The instructions for the ensemble version (and this is also the preface printed – to my mind erroneously – in the 2-piano version) say that there should be occasional loud sounds, which might infer lifting the left pedal, but as it is still possible to play louder sounds while using it, in the end this would be a decision about tone colour more than anything else.

The unpublished foreword for Tudor states 'dynamics are free', so loud sounds would not need to be occasional, making the use of the left pedal even more of a colour related decision than one pertaining to dynamics. This also implies that the research on tone quality that I mentioned in the previous section would not be the whole story, and one might refer more to Tudor's 1958 recording of *Intersection 3* to hear the sound that he brought to these pieces.

Of particular interest is the recording used of *Ixion* by the Cunningham Dance Company for their performances of *Summerspace*. This performance of the 2-piano version played by John Cage and David Tudor, was recorded for rehearsals while on tour with the Cunningham Dance Company in Stockholm, most probably in October 1958,[33] and was also used in the film *Summerspace*, directed by Charles Atlas that documented the performance. [34]

Summerspace was not performed at that tour as this was a trip consisting of only Cage, Tudor, Cunningham and Carolyn Brown.[35]

There are quite a few elements in this rendition that shine a very interesting light on how one might approach the 2-piano version. The overall amplitude of the performance is very low, and no real loud sounds are heard anywhere. This would not be in line with the instructions for the ensemble version, which are after all printed in the published score, but perfectly fine when using the (unpublished) specific piano preface, which states notes can be of any dynamic. Choosing to only play quiet sounds therefore would be perfectly acceptable.

Rhythmically the performance is kept quite regular, with a generally slow pace, and only occasionally some busier moments are heard. There are a lot of repetitions of short chromatic lines and the overall melodic and harmonic character has a consistency in line with Feldman's other works of the time. Pedalling is generous, which takes away most of the particular kind of pointillism one might expect. In addition, the pedal is often held for long stretches of time, resulting in sounds being extended way beyond the length of one box. Occasionally there are more crystalline sounding sections where no or little pedal is used, and they seem to be related to the kind of movement the dance is displaying at the time. If this is the case this would imply the music following the dance rather than the other way round, but I have not been able to find any kind of link between the two, which would be completely in line with the way Merce Cunningham worked, having a complete independence between music and dance.

One very interesting change is that the performance ends with the part marked 'low', which means that only 397 of the 745 boxes, or 53.29% of the piece, are used.

The performance takes 20'35" in total, with the rendition of *Ixion* coming in at 20'20", which is definitely not in line with the ca. 11 minutes the published score states – something that might or might not have come from Feldman but could also have been added later by the publisher – and is even longer than the '15 to 17 minutes' Cunningham said it would last. If the score would be performed in full then the tempo would be about MM 37 per box, but if indeed the piece ends at the end of the first system of page 3 of the score, the tempo falls to a very slow MM 19, or a little over 3 seconds per box.

What would be the conclusion drawn from examining this performance? The recording was done by two performers who were closer to Feldman than anyone else at the time and we can quite safely assume it had his approval. However, given the very open nature of the score it would be unwise to take Cage and Tudor's performance as the ultimate and only benchmark, thereby limiting or negating the amount of freedom the notation gives to the performers. However, the recording could help in establishing an aesthetic framework within which one could develop one's own performance. In addition, this recording shows that there are elements in the score, such as the use of pedal, that are not mentioned per se, without this implying there should be no use whatsoever. The absence of an indication does not imply a total absence of use.

Even though it is risky to take performance instructions from one piece and applying them onto another, there is an interesting sentence in the preface to the 1959 graph piece *Atlantis*, a work for either 17 or 10 players, that might be able to tell us something about how to approach the 2-piano version. The score tells us that:

> Piano is notated to be played in the high, middle or low register, similar in style to "Last Pieces". [36]

Last Pieces are a set of four pieces, also written in 1959, for piano solo, but written in a more conventional notational style, albeit only specifying pitches, not rhythm. The instructions for the movements specify dynamics (soft, soft as possible), tempo (slow, fast, very slow, very fast) and tell the performer 'Durations are free', or 'Durations are free for each hand' (piece 4). [37] These performance instructions would not be of much use when applying them to either *Ixion* or *Atlantis*, where the tempo is either given (*Atlantis*) or unclear (*Ixion*), and duration is dictated by the box structure and the dynamics are specified in the preface to the score. It will also not help us in determining use of pedal as this is not indicated anywhere in *Last Pieces*, so we would have to take this instruction in a different way.

I would suggest Feldman might have wanted to say something about the choice of sounds that should go into the piano part, telling the pianist to have a look at the score of *Last Pieces* to be informed about harmony, density and an overall sense of progression and pitch. The various movements have different densities, from 2- to 4-note aggregates in no. 1 and 3, single notes to 9-note aggregates in no. 2, whereby in no. 4 things get unclear due to the instruction that the hands should be independent from each other. Four-note aggregates are the maximum in the right hand with the left having one 5-note chord. It is also interesting to see that a lot of the chords are not possible to be performed without either rolling or breaking them (the difference being that in breaking a chord one keeps the part that can be played with one hand together with the rest of the chord sounding as an appoggiatura. As there are a few arpeggio signs in no. 4 it would be logical to assume the other chords that are too large for one hand need to be broken in some way, but there is no specific instruction. The harmonies and intervals avoid any kind of tonal allusions and do not have any apparent harmonic progression. There are occasional moments where for example two C naturals sound together, usually, with a few octaves distance, but these do not function as tonal elements. The overall impression is that there is a great variety of register, preferring larger leaps in both hands.

In both *Atlantis* and *Ixion* the amount of sounds (pitches) to be played in each box is given, leaving the harmonic and intervallic language to be the main thing to learn from the score of *Last Pieces*. I would argue that the instruction found in *Atlantis* is very helpful for *Ixion*, at least as far as the 2-piano version is concerned. It is a lot less helpful for the ensemble version, because even though the overall pitch choices could very well be influenced by looking at *Last Pieces*, this would ultimately only be valid for the piano part, which is just one out of ten parts in *Ixion*.

Some thoughts about personal performance choices would not be out of place at this point and the suggestions I will give in the next section of this chapter are strategies I have implemented when working on various graph pieces.

Thinking about general approaches to a score is not quite the same as having to actually make choices for one's own performance. The most basic decision that would need to be made is whether or not I would make a version of the piece in advance, as David Tudor was wont to do. The concept of the notation implies that the composer expects the choice of pitch and other vital decisions to be made on the spot by the performer. Therefore, I would not fix anything that should remain unfixed.

One question that could arise is whether or not the scores as presented is the clearest possible notation or if one might consider re-notating the piece in a way that might make more sense to the performer.

This is what Cage did with the instrumental parts, just to make them more easily readable to musicians who are not used to alternative notations, but for someone who has had a lot of experience reading graphic and other non-standard scores I would decide to leave the score as it is.

This would entail that I would need to spend quite some time getting intimately acquainted with the notation, time that would be combined with finding out the practicalities of choosing the actual pitches.

This in itself requires some thought: how conscious should a performer be about which notes to play? Would it be acceptable to simply follow the instructions on register, and once one's hands are in the general area, not think too much about which keys are depressed as long as it is the correct amount?

I would say that ultimately this might be the desired way forward, but in order to get there one needs to make sure that the problems the score throws at you are thoroughly internalised. This would involve developing strategies on conscious and unconscious decision-making and the main element would need to be density and number of notes per box. If we look at the score of the 2-piano version, we see that the highest number used is 18 (the 8th box in III^{6}) which is clearly more than can be played with 10 fingers and so some thought needs to be given on how to deal with numbers greater than 10.

The instructions tell us that we need to play as many single notes as possible, which implies that chords should be used sparingly, a rule that clearly has not been followed by Cage and Tudor in their 1958 recording. Depending on the tempo chosen by the performers it is totally conceivable that a performance can be done without needing to play any chords at all, although this is not likely for those icti where more than one box of the three contains a number, that will involve shifting position, something that will take some time and therefore takes away time from pressing keys.

The faster the tempo, the more difficult it will be to keep just playing single notes. This does not yet take into consideration the process of choosing the actual pitches. Even though a more or less chance-based system would be desirable, this will only work if one would take time, if necessary, to have a level of control over the shape and position of one's hands. Most pianists will have the standard tonal repertoire as their base, and this means that the hand falls almost automatically into positions that form major and minor triads.

As we saw earlier in this chapter, even though it is not mentioned explicitly in the performance instructions, one might need to adhere to Feldman's harmonic language, which does not usually feature tonal chords at all but is more geared towards more dissonant intervals like sevenths, seconds and tritones, even though he often makes use of octaves as well. One might need to work on making these intervals therefore the natural hand shape rather to make sure Feldman's harmonies and intervals are favoured without too much conscious effort.

The next stage in practicing would be to take small segments of the score, a few icti at the time, and try out various ways of filling the space/time with sounds. This is not too complicated if there is only one box to play, but if there are two or three this quickly becomes quite tricky.

If we look at the first few icti of the score we see that piano 1 starts with a single box to be filled with 5 sounds. This is easy enough, but the next ictus sees all three boxes filled with 7, 3, and 4 respectively. Here it would be beneficial to take this single ictus and try out a number of versions, making different choreographies for the two hands to see what feels natural, what feels possible and to get used to the idea of shifting positions quickly. Initially, I would recommend doing this in no particular tempo but taking it as slow as needed, and to speed up bit by bit until the desired tempo is reached.

An additional complication is that nowhere does it say within the score that a number in any box needs to be completed as one unit, and it is quite possible to combine numbers so that, for example, one plays 3 sounds from the top box, before playing 2 from the lowest, then 1 from the middle, 2 more from the lowest, 2 from the top, 2 from the middle and, finally, the remaining 2 from the top.

As is immediately clear, this adds an extra layer of complication to the performance, as it not only involves more shifting of the hands, but also necessitates more thinking and counting to make sure one plays the correct number of sounds. Therefore, it would be safe to assume that unless a version is made beforehand, in which case it is easy enough to shift between registers, most players would play the required amount of notes in one box as one entity.

The instructions given to Tudor state that performers need to play single notes as much as possible. This should be practical for most of the piece, as there should not be problems playing single notes when only one box is filled, and in those icti where there are two or three boxes to be articulated we see that for the overall majority of cases these numbers do not exceed 7. Only very occasionally, and especially in the last section of the piece from III^{13} onwards, do we see some larger numbers superimposed. Here it would be practical to add some chords, even though with enough practice this could still be kept to a minimum. It will be up to the individual performer to decide how they would decide on the amount of chordal material to use, as there is no clear indication other than 'as many single notes as possible', which is open to interpretation according to a player's individual capabilities. Besides, the specific instructions for the 2-piano version are not published in the score so there is no reason to assume knowledge of these when performing the piece. Even so, the instructions for the ensemble version do say that the piano plays simultaneous sounds only if there are too many single sounds to play, which is in effect the same instruction.

When practicing I would suggest focusing initially on those icti that have more than one layer to get the thought process and the act of jumping from one part of the register to another in one's muscle memory, and starting with short excerpts, under tempo, to get used to the process of having to decide both pitches and rhythm on the spot. Then one might want to string a number of short fragments together into longer ones, until the whole of the piece can be played in one uninterrupted flow. With regards to rhythm it would be advisable to look at Feldman's use in pieces written around the same time as *Ixion*, and it will be clear that one might want to refrain from using rhythmical elements that are too well-defined and have too much of a regular character. It is rare therefore for Feldman's music to contain too many regular beats or subdivisions; the overall rhythmic identity of most of his compositions has a more free and floating feeling.

The next part of the performance preparation is synchronisation of the two piano parts. Here is where a lot of work undertaken could be thrown into chaos again. As described earlier in this chapter, the nature of the notation makes the synchronisation of the 2-piano parts very difficult indeed without some kind of visual or aural clue, either given by one of the performers or by a device functioning as time keeper. The unpredictability of the score makes it impossible to keep track of the other part with any kind of certainty so relying on audible musical clues, as is the standard practice when playing chamber music, is not practical. Once a visual or aural click track has been put in place the synchronisation of the two parts is not problematic and the rehearsals can be used primarily to work on finding a shared tone quality and approach to the performance rules. It is entirely possible to leave matters such as dynamics and the ratio of single notes to aggregates, use of pedal, up to the individual performer and this would work if the pianists know each other well, but it would be advantageous to the musical outcome if some agreement is in place to balance out all the elements.

The recording that Cage and Tudor made is an interesting document and can serve as a good guide to the overall sound world that might need to be in place. However, it needs to be taken into consideration that this version, apart from being only a partial performance, not a complete one, seems to ignore some of the instructions given in either version of the score. Dynamics are constantly low, which is not contrary to the specific 2-piano preface, which merely states dynamics are free, so playing only quiet sounds is fine, although it would be contrary to the instruction in the ensemble preface to play occasional loud sounds. There is, however, a strong preponderance of chordal material, which is not in line with either preface. It is unknown if Feldman approved of this recording for use for the performances of the dance, but it would be almost unthinkable for the recording to be used without the composer's blessing.

Therefore, we should consider this performance to be a valid rendition of the score, although the issue of it being incomplete does throw up some additional questions for which the answers are impossible to arrive at with any kind of certainty. Is the performance incomplete because the 2-piano version had not yet been finished or was it a conscious choice by the performers, and if so, why? As the performance fits the timing of the dance perfectly and the tempo has been lowered to fit the time necessary it is clear the choices will have been made deliberately. We could conclude from this that the performance instructions as given by Feldman are to be taken seriously, but that there is some leeway, at least for those performers who have enough of a personal connection with the composer.

One possible reason for not adhering to the instructions could lie in the fact that the specific preface for the 2-piano version was not given to Tudor until 1960, more than a year after the recording was made, so these might not yet have been available.

I would look at the Cage/Tudor recording therefore as an interesting piece of performance history of *Ixion*, but not necessarily as an example for other players to follow except as a rendition that is perfectly in line with Feldman's general harmonic, intervallic, and stylistic language.

A recording of *Ixion*, coincidentally also in Stockholm, made by Scholz & Persson,[38] is a lot more in line with the preface, although the use of dynamics might indicate that they did not have access to the specific 2-piano instructions done for Tudor, and the character of the piece is highly virtuosic, pointillistic and scintillating. However, it is clear that the performance was done without any thought for the dance it is supposed to accompany, as the tempo chosen is so high that the complete piece takes only 7 minutes and 30 seconds, instead of the 20 minutes the choreography lasts. NB: There is a duration of 11 minutes given on the first page of the score, but it is unclear where this length comes from, and there is no indication of duration in the score of the ensemble version at all. I would say this in itself is not a problem as it is entirely appropriate to view the piece as a standalone rather than strictly a dance piece, and since there is no tempo indication in the score there would be no reason to say their high-speed rendition would be wrong. It would, however, be one of the few examples of a dance score that when used as a concert piece takes on a totally different identity.

All these observations are written with the 2-piano version of *Ixion* in mind, but a lot of the ideas could be transposed onto the ensemble version as well.

There some caveats though: the individual parts of the ensemble version only have one single register layer, so the difficulty of mixing different registers does not come into play, making it a lot easier to keep one's bearings. There would not be any significant coordination problems as in all likelihood there would be a conductor functioning as a visual timekeeper, and as someone who would oversee and work on the particularities of choosing the appropriate pitch material, and generally keep an eye and ear on the performers to make sure they adhere to the performance instructions.

Ixion
and Jackson Pollock

The painter that Feldman acknowledges as a major influence on the graph pieces in general and *Ixion* in particular, specifically with regards to the way the two versions of *Ixion* are composed, is Jackson Pollock.

Feldman got to know Pollock in 1951, when he was asked to write music for a film that Hans Namuth made in 1950. Namuth's first plan was to use Balinese Gamelan music but Pollock felt the film needed music that was more American. Pollock's wife, the painter Lee Krasner, then approached John Cage. However, as Cage later told Irving Sadler, "I couldn't abide Pollock's work because I couldn't stand the man." He recalled elsewhere, Pollock "was generally so drunk, and he was actually an unpleasant person for me to encounter. I remember seeing him on the same side of the street as I was, and I would always cross over to the other side." [...] Cage refused Krasner's request but referred her to Feldman, who accepted it in return for an ink drawing."[1] Feldman wrote a score for two cellos, which was performed by Daniel Stern, playing both parts.

Namuth wanted to photograph and film Pollock at work, and first shot some black and white footage, but felt that making a colour film was a more appropriate way of documenting the painter's way of working. He filmed Pollock painting on a large sheet of glass the work that was to become *Number 29*, 1950, so that all possible viewpoints could be used. According to most sources the idea of having him paint on glass does seem to originate from Namuth, although in a 1978 interview (the interviewer has so far not been identified) Krasner remembers that it was just something Pollock wanted to try:

> BR: It was Namuth's idea that he should paint on glass.
>
> LK: Was it? I was there while Pollock painted it, certainly. But I wasn't there when Namuth suggested that he paint on glass. As far as I'm concerned, Jackson got a sheet of glass, and decided to paint on it, and Namuth photographed it. [...] The first I heard of it, Pollock showed me a piece of glass. When I asked him what it was for, he said he wanted to try to paint on it. As you know, he was constantly experimenting. I always thought he got the idea of painting on glass from Duchamp.[2]

In a discussion with the Dutch social scientist and music critic Frits Lagerwerff, Feldman talks about how Pollock's way of painting made him see how he could approach composition in a less temporally linear way:

> There are two types of art as a young man in New York that did influence me and they paralleled at the same time. The first was Jackson Pollock. Those years that I was doing the

> graph music. I think the term is "all over". Did you see that early film that I wrote the music for, Pollock, 1951 film, you would see him walking around. That influenced me a lot. And what I did in the graph thing is to break the notion of a cause and effect continuity. What I was looking for was a more… unchanging image, where you have this image and there is movement and mobility but essentially, it's just the energy of keeping up the same image, so to speak. And Pollock influenced me tremendously, and my graph music was very close insofar as that I would be working, say, with the right hand the retrograde on time and I would be going this way [makes a gesture] at the same time. What I liked about it in a sense is that I could see the retrograde without having any notes, just a retrograde of action. That fact that it went linear when it was all finished was another story. But in its composition a retrograde of action took place. So I could be all over, and I used the term "sensitizing" this particular all-time space. And Pollock in a way taught me how to keep motion going, at the same time understanding the nature of stasis.[3]

Christian Wolff also talked about how Feldman would even adopt elements of how Pollock, and most painters, would work:

> I think this interest had to do with his interest in painting. He used to put sheets of graph paper on the wall, and work on them like paintings. Slowly his notation would accumulate, and from time to time he'd stand back to look at the overall design. For him it had less to do with belief in chance: it was more function than anything else. He would talk about different weights of sound – and that

> was simply the easiest way to express them. Pitches didn't really matter, as there were so many other controls, and he used chance without its interfering with expression.[4]

In an interview he gave 23 years later Wolff restates it as:

> Feldman used to work by putting his manuscripts on the wall so that he could step back and look at them the way an artist looks at a picture. I'm not sure about this, but I have a feeling sometimes he might have thought of something to do "down here", and then go back "up here". It was really like a canvas rather than a linear, narrative structure.[5]

The manuscript of the ensemble version of *Ixion* is written on 12 leaves, or rather: "12 strips of paper cut from a writing pad, whose measurements are partly 3.7 cm x 28. 2 cm (height per width), and partly 11 cm x 28 cm.[6] This would indicate that the empty grid structure would be of such a size that it would have been easy enough to have it affixed to the wall for a total overview of the canvas. The strips would each contain one or more systems and we can speculate therefore that the canvas would have been a larger overall surface rather than one long horizontal strip, which would be in line with the idea of looking at the whole score as one painterly canvas. The size of the strips did surprise me somewhat in that they are the same as the published score, and that they are quite small, even though the numbers are legible for someone with decent eyesight. However, Feldman's eyes were notoriously bad and he needed to get up very close to the paper to get the notation in focus. This may suggest that Feldman would have been more involved with the overall look and feel of the whole canvas than with the smaller details as he viewed the grid structure from further away.

Feldman himself describes the parallels between his own way of thinking and Pollock's, but more as something they both shared than as something Feldman learned from Pollock, even though at other times he did acknowledge being heavily influenced by him:

> Soon after meeting Rauschenberg I met Jackson Pollock, who asked me to write music for a film about him that had just been completed. I was very pleased about this since it was just the very beginning of my career. Pollock lived way out on Long Island and only came to the city sporadically, making it very difficult to establish a real continuity to our relationship. In thinking back to that time, I realize now how much the musical ideas I had in 1951 paralleled his mode of working. Pollock placed his canvas on the ground and painted as he walked around it. I put sheets of graph paper on the wall, each sheet framed the same time duration and was, in effect, a visual rhythmic structure. What resembled Pollock was my "allover" approach to the time-canvas. Rather than the usual left-to-right passage across the page, the horizontal squares of the graph paper represented the tempo – with each box being equal to a preestablished ictus; and the vertical squares were the instrumentation of the composition.[7]

Pollock's practice of painting with the canvas lying on the floor started around 1946, and there are some statements by Pollock about why this change came about, although Krasner was unsure about why he changed from working in the more conventional way of having the canvas upright to having it horizontal. She says in the 1978 interview:

> I don't have the remotest idea of why he wanted to work on the floor. [...] The only thing I remember hearing was that he had seen the Indian sand painters working on the ground. [...] I only remember hearing about the [Navajo] Indian sand paintings from him in terms of a precedent for working on the ground.[8]

Pollock started to drip the paint on the canvas rather than painting in a standard way with brushes – he used all manner of sticks which he dipped in the paint or enamel, and then would let the paint drip down. What is quite peculiar about this horizontal way of painting is that, according to Krasner:

> [...] it is working in the air and knowing where it will land.[9]

Pollock thought that easel painting was dying and started to get away from the traditional painter's implements more and more until in 1947 he only painted on unstretched canvases lying flat. He words it in a statement written for the only existing edition of what was going to be the periodical *Possibilities*, edited by Robert Motherwell and Harold Rosenberg, and published in New York in the winter of 1947/48:

> My painting does no come from the easel. I hardly ever stretch my canvas before painting. I prefer to tack the unstretched canvas to the hard wall or floor. I need the resistance of a hard surface. On the floor I am more at ease. I feel nearer, more a part of the painting, since this way I

> can walk around it, work from the four sides and literally be in the painting.[10]

According to Clement Greenberg:

> There was something about getting away from that contained box thing [of the cabinet painting] which is one reason Pollock painted on unstretched canvas and why he painted so big from time to time. He wanted to find his way to the edges of the picture rather than start out with them – without those edges being given, as he would have been on an unstretched canvas.[11]

Pollock's way of working led the art theorist and critic Harold Rosenberg to coin the term 'action painting'. He describes the mindset as:

> The painter no longer approached his easel with an image in his mind; he went up to it with material in his hand to do something to that other piece of material in front of him. The image would be the result of this encounter.[12]
>
> The big moment came when it was decided to paint… just TO PAINT. The gesture on the canvas was a gesture of liberation, from Value – political, esthetic, moral.[13]

This mindset on paper looks like Rosenberg expects the artist not to think about what they are doing, but to look upon painting as a spontaneous act. Even though Rosenberg had some misgivings about Pollock's paintings and the hype surrounding his work, which grew to almost mythical proportions, the term 'action painter' seemed almost coined for Pollock, and Rosenberg called him a 'major model'. He felt that Willem de Kooning was a much more important figure in American painting, whereas Clement Greenberg, who was in a life-long state of professional conflict with Rosenberg, thought Pollock the pinnacle of Abstract Expressionist painting – up to the early 1950s at any rate, after which Greenberg lost a lot of his admiration for Pollock, calling his later work "forced, pumped, dressed up."[14] Greenberg did not agree with the term 'action painting' anyway and was much more involved with the idea of modern painting as a means of destroying the concept of 'easel painting'. He described how modern painters:

> Render every element, every part of the canvas equivalent; and they likewise wave the work of art into a tight mesh whose principle of formal unity is contained and recapitulated in each thread, so that we find the essence of the whole work in every one of its parts.[15]

Greenberg used the alternate term 'all-over painting' to describe the paintings of Mark Tobey, stating that he was

> The first painter to arrive at "all-over" design, covering the picture surface with an even, largely undifferentiated system of uniform motifs that cause the result to look as though it could be continued indefinitely beyond the frame like a wallpaper pattern.[16]

Tobey was one of John Cage's favourite painters, but Feldman hardly ever mentions him, and Tobey, living in Seattle most of his life, was not a part of the "Cedar Street Tavern" crowd. Greenberg was, to a certain extent, a kind of outsider member of this group of painters (with Feldman as the only composer), tolerated but put in his place whenever it felt needed. As Feldman recalls:

> One evening, when I was still a newly arrived immigrant at the Cedar Bar, Elaine and Willem de Kooning casually took my arm as they passed, and said, "Come on over to Clem Greenberg's". There were just a few people when we got there. After a while I found myself listening to Greenberg, who was talking about Cézanne. De Kooning showed signs of impatience and seemed to be trying to control his anger. He finally broke out with "One more word about Cézanne, and I'll punch you in the nose!" Greenberg, very startled, had been saying only very intelligent and perceptive things. It was hard for him to understand that what De Kooning resented was his having ideas on the matter at all. "You have no right to talk about Cézanne", De Kooning snapped. "Only I have the right to talk about Cézanne.[17]

Feldman agreed with Greenberg about the term 'Action Painting' being problematic:

> Personally, I have never understood the term "Action Painting" as a description of the work of the fifties. The closest I can come to its meaning is that the painter tries for a less predeterminate structure. [...] My quarrel with the term "Action Painting" is that it gave rise to the erroneous idea that the painter, now being "free", could do "anything he liked". But it is not true that the more one is free, the more things one has to choose from. Actually, it is the academician who has the alternatives. Freedom is best understood by someone like Rothko, who was free to do

> only one thing – to make a Rothko – and did so over and over again.[18]

In his essay written for an LP with eight pieces from the 1950s, among which two graph scores, *Projection 4* and *Intersection 3*, Frank O'Hara describes the link between some of Pollock's all-over paintings, Webern's serial pieces and by extension, Feldman's music. However, he warns us that "… these analogies cease to be helpful if carried too far".[19]

Since *Ixion's* compositional concept to a large degree has to do with trying to capture some of Pollock's way of 'overall' painting, another possible way of looking at the difference between the two versions would be a purely visual one.

If one would try and analyse the work more as shapes on canvas (or paper), perhaps this would give us some other idea of Feldman's transference of material from one instrumentation to the other.

As a first stage, to see if anything useful would come out if this, I endeavoured to make what, for want of a better term, could be called a 'Pollockised' score, where, as logically as I could, I connected the numbers to form flowing lines. This in itself turned out to be of very limited use; even though the result could be said to have some sort of vague resemblance to some of Pollock's less dense and more monochrome paintings,[20] there is nothing to suggest that this was in any way on Feldman's mind (Fig. 16).

Furthermore, it turned out that contrary to what one might assume, the same procedure applied to the 2-piano version results in an even less dense structure with hardly any discernible links to Pollock's practice (Fig. 17). I would say that this is an example of taking the analogy too far and that the link with Pollock's painting would need to be found in a more indirect, perhaps metaphorical way of thinking about density, structure, movement and compositional shape.

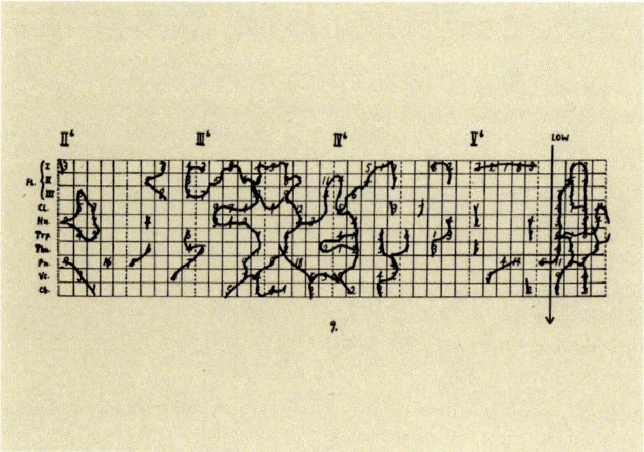

FIGURE 16

John Snijders, *Pollockised version of Ixion*, ensemble version, page 9 (2018).

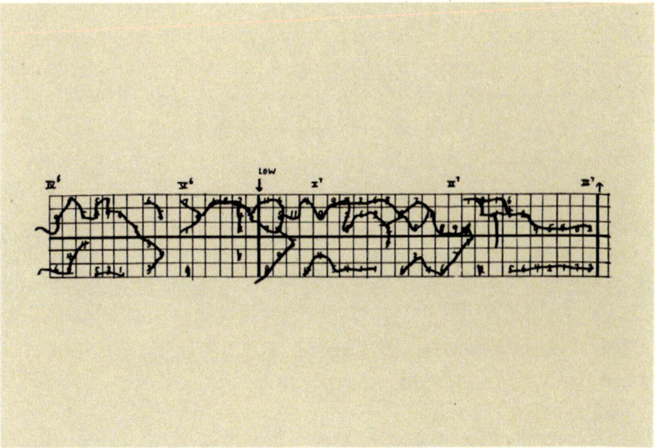

FIGURE 17

John Snijders, *Pollockised version of Ixion*, 2-piano version, page 3 (2018).

Feldman's remark about being too design-oriented in the earlier graph pieces could help us in coming up with some thoughts about the decision-making processes involved.

It seems that for the graph scores there was a mix between the visual and aural, but it could well be that there was more of an emphasis on the visual in the graph pieces from the 1950s. However, it would be problematic to say the least to think that sound, and more specifically colour, would be of less importance than scores mainly 'looking beautiful'. In addition, this way of looking at the piece system by system might not correlate with the view, supported by the measurements of the manuscript, that the total surface area of the piece would have been seen as one uninterrupted canvas.

A possible relationship between *Ixion* and Pollock's work lies in the idea of dealing with time.

Here we will need to distinguish between music being an inherently time-based art form, simply meaning that it takes a more or less set time to listen to a piece of music, and painting being in effect a stationary art. Of course, it does take time to look at a painting, but the amount of time is not prescribed and can range from anything from a cursory glance to an extended in-depth scrutiny of the work, looking at all the minute details, brush strokes, colour hues, overall composition, etc.

For a listener it is only possible to discover further detail through repeated listening or by zooming in on specific details by reading the score or listening to one or more performances. Going back and listening to a specific fragment again is something that cannot be done other than when using a recording and is not a common occurrence for anyone but musicians, composers and musicologists, whereas lingering on a specific detail in any work of non-time-based visual art is quite normal.

That is the time element from an audience perspective, but it is not the only way in which the two disciplines differ with respect to dealing with temporal issues. As music moves in time a composer will usually be focused on the straight temporal journey of the piece and by extension, the listener's journey too. A painter though has to consider the overall structure of the canvas in a more overall way of thinking, as the viewer can make their own journey across the surface and decide on what to focus on, where to look next and which parts to completely ignore.

Feldman might have thought about a way of composing *Ixion* that is closer to this overall idea of structure, perhaps even ignoring the idea that a piece of music will need to have some kind of logic from one moment to the next, but in the end, even when the act of composition would reflect this, you will inevitably end up with a score that still adheres to the usual traditional directionality that any piece of music will have. The composition might be done in a similar way to Pollock's painting technique, but the listener will listen to it in a traditionally linear way, just as Cunningham's dance unfolds linearly in time, and will while listening in no way be aware of the specific ideas that Feldman might have had about emulating the painter's way of working.

Another way of looking at the way time might behave in the two disciplines focuses not on the listener but on the creator. At the risk of sounding overly simplistic, both composing and painting take time, although in general composing music is a far slower process than painting. There are exceptions to this rule of course, and there are composers who can write pieces in a few days or less, even though this seems to be associated more with the Baroque and Classical era than most music composed post-1800. It is not uncommon for composers nowadays to take months, sometimes years to complete a piece of music, and we are not necessarily talking about large-scale works here.

Painting by comparison seems to be a lot quicker in its process of creation, with painters like Howard Hodgkin, who often took years before he decided a work was finished, being the exception that proves the rule. Feldman was not an especially slow composer but compared with the work process of his painter friends composing did take quite a lot more time.

Pollock on the other hand mostly worked in a state of excited but controlled frenzy and paintings would more often than not be painted in one go over a relatively short period. This would be quite an important distinction when we compare the way *Ixion* was composed to the way Pollock's paintings were done: even if Feldman would try to emulate Pollock's work process it could not have been done with the same kind of energy and speed but would have been a much more deliberate and slower process.

However, my idea would be that Feldman was not so much interested in the speed with which Pollock worked, but more the formal aspects of how to deal with the totality of the canvas and how to fill it with marks, or in music, sounds.

The usual methodology in composing would be to know in some detail what the overall shape of the piece would be. Now this was already something Feldman was not really interested in and he would often write without a preconceived formal plan, and get from one moment to the next, usually in a very linear way, starting at the beginning and making his way through the piece until he felt the piece was finished.

There are sketches for some pieces, even though Feldman maintained he did not make sketches – something that could have to do with a need for some kind of self-mythologizing – but these seem to be mostly centred around searching for harmonies and intervallic ideas, not around formal aspects of pieces.

If we compare this to Pollock's way of painting, where there could well be an initial idea of how the finished form/structure of the canvas would look like, not in detail but in the overall idea of the composition, the actual filling of the surface area would not be a linear process at all. He would go from one part of the canvas to a disconnected one, adding things here and there, a way of working that could have been taken from Cézanne more than anyone else. Cézanne would often work in a seemingly haphazard way on his paintings where bits would be left unfinished for a bit, then worked on later, working on other parts of the canvas in between, but always with a strong sense of overall control over the form and image.

The notion that the overall structure of the work, where all parts are seen as equally important resulting in a need for every element of the composition to speak to every other element was of great importance to the Abstract Expressionists and was something they freely admitted to learning from Cézanne.

Feldman seems to have taken this way of working for *Ixion*, where the overall canvas, in the form of the full set of grid pages, would be visible at all times and where he would add things here and there, working in a completely non-linear way. This is according to Christian Wolff in his descriptions of Feldman's method of working quoted earlier in this chapter.[21] As Dore Ashton puts it:

> His music [...] refuses the architectural tradition of music and aligns itself with the expansive space of contemporary painting.[22]

For a composer to look at the act of composing in this completely non-linear way is quite a courageous step to take. It means that you forego the idea of thinking about a piece of music as a form that needs one specific logical narrative with a compositional method that will make sure you keep a constant control over form and structure. It would have been a logical and even necessary step for Feldman to explore ways of composing that would get rid of the logic of the linear narrative that had been the standard feature of music composition until then, and, influenced by Cage's thinking more than anyone else's, make music that would sound:

> As if you're not listening but looking at something in nature.[23]

This change in formal thinking would have been made easier with a change away from the standard system of music notation to enable a different kind of thinking about time and structure and it would therefore have been a logical step to devise some sort of alternative notational system, one that would accommodate a more discontinuous way of working and would also allow for the kind of 'all-over' approach Feldman wanted to achieve.

Looking at the way time plays in the act of creating a painting or a composition is not the only comparison we can try to make. A more general look at how both artists viewed the work process reveals some interesting parallels. The idea expressed by a remark by the Spanish painter Juan

Gris, printed in the foreword of Motherwell and Rosenberg's short-lived periodical *Possibilities* can be seen as very relevant to both Feldman's and Pollock's way of working:

> You are lost the instant you know what the result will be.[24]

This reverberates in the anecdote Cage told when Feldman came to visit him for the first time early in 1950 and showed him the score of a string quartet he just finished. Cage asked Feldman how he had made it, to which the rather meek reply was "I don't know how I made it", causing great joy to Cage.[25] Pollock said something that could be seen as being in a similar vein:

> When I am in my painting, I'm not aware of what I'm doing.[26]

This idea of having confidence in one's instincts was of vital importance for both Feldman and Pollock and would most likely have been an additional reason for Feldman to feel some kind of connection. Some caution is necessary though: it would be problematic to go too far in equating the ways these non-conscious decisions could be made in Pollock's painting practice and Feldman's composing. The 'automatism' that Pollock allowed, giving over to an only partial control of his movements and thoughts during the act of painting is certainly not on the same level as Feldman's 'not knowing' when composing. Even when he would not know how he made the specific decisions, they were never done with any kind of automatism, but the result of a very deliberate process of controlling the material. There is no reason to assume that Feldman would have given up this control when working on the graph pieces, and even though there was no specification as to pitch and often rhythm, the form and shape of the pieces show a clear deliberate thinking about structure.

Even in *Ixion*, where it seems that a lot of elements are defined by more intuitive decision making it is clear that there are quite a few moments in the piece where a very specific kind of choice was made. The insert of a short passage of low sounds, a page and a half where almost every box has the number 1, the ever-growing density towards the end, working to a perhaps near classical climax, I firmly believe that all of these characteristics are the result of conscious choices, not the kind of quasi *écriture automatique* Pollock might seem to have employed.

For one, the simple act of writing down the marks is necessarily a far slower process than pouring and dripping paint on the canvas, as they need multiple small acts and decisions, not sweeping gestures.

I would conclude that the way Feldman emulated Pollock's way of working was more involved with the look of the finished score than the process of non-linear composing, trying to find a compositional 'all-over' equivalent. In this I would say Feldman did succeed, but this does not mean the sounding result is close to the visual identity of a work by Pollock. The concerns and links lie more in the thought processes rather than the musical outcome.

Conclusion

Drawing conclusions after having studied any score, especially concerning performance practice and other non-analytical elements, is always difficult, and one ends up with opinions and cautious attempts at expressing ideas about something that is to a large extent inexpressible in words. When faced with a score as open as *Ixion* this task is even trickier. Nevertheless, there are some issues that I have encountered, some more general in nature, some going more into finer details of the score and its performance, that can be taken as my personal view on how to deal with the various problems performers will encounter and the decisions needed to come to a meaningful rendition of the notation.

I feel it can be safely said that Feldman devised a truly new way of notating music, and that we might go as far as calling him the inventor of graphic score notation. But as often is the case with pioneers, he was not able to catch all the musical issues he wanted to address to his own satisfaction and rather than developing the notation further until it could do what he needed it to do, he simply abandoned it and returned to a more traditional notation. Any kind of innovation cannot work to its full potential if the instructions are not totally clear and unambiguous. Although sometimes ambiguity can be an integral part of the notation, I don't think Feldman's graph scores fall into that category. The reason his prefaces often do not give all the information needed is probably a combination of the fact that most of these pieces would have been composed for close friends and collaborators who would be able to ask Feldman to clarify anything that wasn't clear, and the composer not being the most precise notator anyway, both in his graph and non-graph pieces. This led to John Cage expressing his frustration with the way the early graph pieces were written down and offering to copy them out neatly, which he did with two of them, *Intersection 2* and *Projection 4*. Feldman clearly took Cage's criticism to heart and the later graph scores are a lot more consistent and clearer in their notation. Even so, *Ixion* suffers from having a preface that leaves a number of elements open, unspecified or simply not clear enough. Tempo is not given, the exact way of how to place sounds in boxes is not entirely clear, and most importantly, the preface printed in the 2-piano version is not correct. Whether this was an oversight on Feldman's part or the publisher's, or both, is not known, but it would help future performances of this version if this could be rectified by replacing the current preface with the proper 2-piano one.

The most contentious subject that I have tried to make sense of is the actual performance practice and practical performance of *Ixion*. It is a perfect example of the problems thrown up by a notational system that leaves decisions up to the performer that can lead to results that the composer deems undesirable. Again, this will be directly related to the aforementioned fact that most of the initial performers would be so well acquainted with Feldman's idiom that they would interpret the scores to the composer's satisfaction, but the problems started as soon as Feldman wrote graph scores for larger forces, where he would no longer be able to rely on knowledgeable or even sympathetic performers.

I have shown that Feldman's ideas about pitch and harmony were a lot less forgiving than those of Cage, and where Cage would be more than happy to accept whatever choices a performer would make, as long as it is within the confines of the rules of the score, Feldman most definitely was not.

In my opinion this makes it necessary, vital even, for any performer who wants to perform any of Feldman's graph scores to do due diligence and research the musical language the piece and composer bring with them.

I have made an analysis of both versions of *Ixion* to try and find out the exact nature of the relationship between them: are they to be seen as two separate pieces, both with their own musical identity, or is the 2-piano version more a piano reduction of the ensemble version?

The conclusion I feel confident to take is that they can be seen as two versions of the same material, but with their own musical identity, enough to treat them as separate compositions in their own right. Due to the nature of the score's performance rules it will often be hardly possible to identify the two versions as the same piece, as the overall identity of the parts is radically different between them.

I have not been able to say with any kind of certainty what Feldman's strategy was to collapse the ten layers of the ensemble version onto the six layers, performed by four hands, of the 2-piano version. He is generally quite consistent in thinning out textures that would be impractically dense for two pianists, but sometimes goes in the opposite direction, and some of the very particular moments in the ensemble score, such as the section where all performers have the number 1 in their boxes, change beyond recognition in the 2-piano version.

I would conclude that the musical and gestural character of the overall sounding result was of less importance than the collapse of the layers and keeping the overall density of the piece as similar as would be practical when reducing the number of performers from between 13 and 19 to 2.

The second part of this book deals with the link that Feldman said exists between *Ixion* and the painterly practice of the American Abstract Expressionists, and specifically that of Jackson Pollock.

It is quite hard to get to the bottom of this as there have not been much more than a few fairly brief statements about this in any of Feldman's writings or talks, and the precise way of how the all-over painting technique of Pollock found its way into the score of *Ixion* is hard to determine. We have anecdotal evidence that the empty score was treated as an empty canvas and that Feldman did not compose this piece in a temporally linear way. The idea of there being a structure of the piece before Feldman started composing the final score is highly debatable, as his ideas about structure and form would usually be highly intuitive and not governed by predetermined choices. This would be in line with Pollock's practice, where the structure of a painting grew out of the making of it rather than being in any way fixed beforehand. However, I think this is more a case of both artists having the same kind of practice to begin with and it would be incorrect to say that Feldman adopted Pollock's way of structuring for *Ixion*. It might be argued that perhaps Feldman's use of orchestral colouring is related to Pollock's use of colours in his paintings and that the idea Feldman had for *Ixion* to be a pointillistic composition but again, no real evidence for this has been found other than some general remarks by Feldman on Pollock's use of primary colours which he found to be related with Mondrian's palette. It is very problematic to determine what primary colours would be in music and I would not want to conclude *Ixion's* orchestration tries to employ these.

References

Introduction
1. Feldman, *Give My Regards to Eighth Street, Collected Writings of Morton Feldman*, p. 144
2. These talks and conversations are collected in Feldman, *Morton Feldman in Middelburg, Lectures and Conversations.*
3. Silverman, *Begin Again, A Biography of John Cage*, p. 255
4. *The Aesthetics of Imperfection in Music and the Arts*, Ed. Hamilton and Pearson, pp. 166-175

Feldman and Composing
1. Feldman, *Give My Regards to Eighth Street, Collected Writings of Morton Feldman*, p. 26
2. ibid., p.33
3. ibid., p. 116
4. Rosenberg, *The Tradition of the New*, p. 32
5. Feldman interviewed by Han Reiziger, VPRO Radio
6. Feldman, *Morton Feldman in Middelburg, Lectures and Conversations*, p. 798
7. Feldman, *Morton Feldman Says: Selected Interviews and Lectures 1964-1987*, p. 197
8. ibid, p. 202
9. Patterson, *Cage and Beyond: an Annotated Interview with Christian Wolff*, p. 72
10. Feldman, *Morton Feldman Says: Selected Interviews and Lectures 1964-1987*, pp. 206-207
11. Feldman interviewed by Han Reiziger, VPRO Radio
12. Greenberg, Clement, *The collected Essays and Criticism, Vol. 4, Modernism with a Vengeance, 1957-1969*, p. 87
13. Cage, Feldman, *Radio Happenings I-VI*, p. 147
14. Philip Guston
15. Feldman interviewed by Han Reiziger, VPRO Radio
16. Feldman, *Essays*, pp. 229-230
17. Feldman, *New Directions in Music 2*, Columbia LP ML5403, 1959
18. Guston, *Collected writings, lectures, and conversations*, p. 97
19. For a complete list, see Appendix
20. Feldman, *Morton Feldman Says: Selected Interviews and Lectures 1964-1987*, p.153

21. Cage, *I-VI,* pp. 238-240 (punctuation, or lack thereof, by Cage)
22. Wolff, *"Taking Chances,"*, p. 66
23. Cage, Feldman, *Radio Happenings I-VI*, p. 17
24. Feldman, *Give My Regards to Eighth Street, Collected Writings of Morton Feldman*, p. 35
25. Cage, *Silence*, p. 158
26. Cage, *A Year From Monday*, p. 31
27. Suzuki, Daisetz Teitaro in http://sweepingzen.com/d-t-suzuki-bio/, accessed 13 July 2018
28. Cage, *The Selected Letters of John Cage*, p. 417
29. Cage, *Silence*, pp. 129-130
30. Feldman, *Morton Feldman Says: Selected Interviews and Lectures 1964-1987*, p. 33
31. ibid., p. 129
32. Feldman, *Give My Regards to Eighth Street, Collected Writings of Morton Feldman*, p. 5
33. ibid., p. 35
34. The Darmstädter Ferienkurse für Neue Musik, which were founded in 1946, are generally seen as the birthplace of strict serialism in 1951.
35. Feldman forgets to include the piano in the instrumental line-up.
36. Feldman, *Give My Regards to Eighth Street, Collected Writings of Morton Feldman*, pp. 5-6
37. ibid., pp. 17-18
38. Oteri, *A Chance Encounter with Christian Wolff, Interview at the Greenwich House Music School, New York*, 11 January 2002, accessed 15-01-2018 https://nmbx.newmusicusa.org/a-chance-encounter-with-christian-wolff/
39. Feldman, *Give My Regards to Eighth Street, Collected Writings of Morton Feldman*, p. 6
40. Feldman, *Essays*, pp. 231-232
41. Work list used is to be found at http://www.cnvill.net/mfworks.pdf
42. Feldman, *Four Instruments*
43. Feldman, *Durations 2*
44. Cline, *The Graph Music of Morton Feldman*
45. Feldman, *Morton Feldman in Middelburg, Lectures and Conversations*, pp. 84-86
46. ibid, 54
47. Feldman, *Morton Feldman Says: Selected Interviews and Lectures 1964-1987*, p. 68
48. Information on dates of exhibitions and works taken from Bois, Joosten, Zander Rudenstine, and Janssen, *Piet Mondrian 1872-1944*
49. Nattiez, *The Boulez-Cage Correspondence*, pp. 114, 116-117
50. Feldman, *Morton Feldman in Middelburg, Lectures and Conversations*, p. 618
51. Greenberg, *The collected Essays and Criticism, Vol. 4, Modernism with a Vengeance, 1957-1969*, p. 247
52. Feldman interviewed by Han Reiziger, VPRO Radio, 5 November 1985, transcription Snijders
53. Feldman, *Morton Feldman Says: Selected Interviews and Lectures 1964-1987*, p. 153

Ixion – History and Scores

1. Cunningham, *Changes; Notes on Choreography*, n.p. (punctuation Cunningham's)
2. Villars (ed.), *Morton Feldman Says: Selected Interviews and Lectures 1964-1987*, p. 65
3. Cage, Feldman, *Radio Happenings I-VI.*, p. 177
4. Higgins, *Greek Myths, A New Retelling*, p. 122

5. The manuscript, held by the Paul Sacher Stiftung in Basel, Switzerland has a different layout. See also Chapter 4, Ixion and Pollock
6. Feldman, *Ixion*, preface (n.p.)
7. Personal correspondence with Patricia Lent of the Merce Cunningham Trust, email of 8 July 2021
8. Feldman, *Ixion*, cond. Jonathan Sheffer, rec. 1996
9. Cline, *The Graph Music of Morton Feldman*, p. 279
10. ibid, pp. 266-269
11. See chapter 1, page 22
12. Feldman interviewed by Han Reiziger, VPRO Radio, 5 November 1985, transcription Snijders

Ixion – performance issues
1. Feldman uses the same feature in the graph score *Atlantis* (1959), but here the low section is only 5 boxes in length.
2. Cunningham, *Changes; Notes on Choreography*, n.p.
3. Cline, *The Graph Music of Morton Feldman*, pp. 203-213
4. Villars (ed.), *Morton Feldman Says: Selected Interviews and Lectures 1964-1987*, pp. 64-65
5. Feldman, *Ixion*, preface
6. Feldman, *Ixion*, preface
7. Silverman, *Begin Again, A Biography of John Cage*, p. 201
8. Cline, *The Graph Music of Morton Feldman*, p. 69
9. ibid, p. 45
10. Feldman does not name the piece, but was probably talking about *Marginal Intersection* for orchestra (1951)
11. Cline, *The Graph Music of Morton Feldman*, p. 45
12. As was pointed out to me by David Connearn, who worked as an assistant to Sol Lewitt (1928-2007) for a number of years, there is a correlation with the way Lewitt's wall drawings are meant to be made by interpreting the instructions given, but that does not mean anyone following the set of rules exactly will necessarily be able to make the drawings in the way Lewitt intended them to be. It takes a lot of specific knowledge of the idiom of mark making and experience in developing a specific kind of handwriting in order to make an acceptable rendition of these works.
13. Cage, *Silence*, p. 10
14. Villars (ed.), *Morton Feldman Says: Selected Interviews and Lectures 1964-1987*, p. 122
15. ibid.
16. Feldman, *Interview with Howard Skempton*
17. Feldman, *Ixion*, cond. Sheffer, recorded 1996, 10'09-10'55"
18. Cage, Feldman, *Radio Happenings I-VI*, p. 181
19 Feldman, *Essays*, p. 156
20. Gregor Piatigorsky, Ukranian-American cellist (1903-1976), Pierre Fournier, French cellist (1906-1986)
21. Feldman, *Give My Regards to Eighth Street, Collected Writings of Morton Feldman*, p. 153
22. Jasha Heifetz, Lithuanian-American violinist (1901-1987)
23. Villars (ed.), *Morton Feldman Says: Selected Interviews and Lectures 1964-1987*, p. 199
24. https://www.youtube.com/watch?v=l2PaI8NvDog (accessed 18 July 2021)
25. https://www.cnvill.net/mffivepianos.htm (accessed 18 July 2021)
26. https://archive.org/details/C_1969_01_24 (accessed 18 July 2021)

27. https://www.cnvill.net/mflindgren.htm (accessed 18 July 2021)
28. Feldman, *For John Cage*
29 David, *The Graph Music of Morton Feldman*, p. 283
30. This is in direct contradiction with the printed preface which says: "dynamics are low with an occasional loud sound".
31. Feldman, *Intersection 2*, p. 1
32. A more extended discussion can be found in David, *The Graph Music of Morton Feldman*, pp. 278-280
33. Feldman, *Ixion*, Cage & Tudor, rec. 1958
34. https://dancecapsules.mercecunningham.org/overview.cfm?capid=46033
35. Personal correspondence with Patricia Lent of the Merce Cunningham Trust, email of 8 July 2021
36. Feldman, *Atlantis*, preface
37. Feldman, *Last Pieces*
38. Feldman, *Ixion*, Scholtz & Persson, rec. 2002

Ixion and Pollock

1. Revill, *The Roaring Silence, John Cage: a Life*, p. 141
2. Krasner, *Interview 27 June 1978*
3. Mörchen, *Morton Feldman in Middelburg, Lectures and Conversations*, pp. 786-788
4. Wolff,"Taking Chances", *Music and Musicians* (May 1969), p. 66-68
5. Patterson, Cage and Beyond: *an Annotated Interview with Christian Wolff*, in *Perspectives of New Music*, Vol. 32, No. 2 (Summer 1992), p. 72
6. Personal correspondence Dr Felix Meyer of the Paul Sacher Stiftung, email dated 13 August 2021
7. Feldman, *Give My Regards to Eighth Street, Collected Writings of Morton Feldman*, p. 147
8. Krasner, *Interview 27 June 1978*, p. 3
9. ibid. p. 7
10. O'Connor, *Jackson Pollock*, pp. 39-40
11. Schreyach, *Pollock's Modernism*, p. 278, n.19
12. Rosenberg, *The Tradition of the New*, p. 25
13. ibid, p. 30
14. Greenberg, *The Collected Essays and Criticism, Vol. 3, Affirmations and Refusals, 1950-1956*, p. 226
15. Greenberg, *The Collected Essays and Criticism, Vol. 2, Arrogant Purpose, 1945-1959*, p. 224
16. Greenberg, *The Collected Essays and Criticism, Vol. 3, Affirmations and Refusals, 1950-1956*, p. 225
17. Feldman, *Give My Regards to Eighth Street, Collected Writings of Morton Feldman*, p. 97
18. ibid, p. 99
19. Kissane (ed.), *Vertical Thoughts, Morton Feldman and the Visual Arts*, p. 87
20. See for example *Number 32* (1950), in the collection of Kunstsammlung Nordrhein-Westfalen, Düsseldorf, Germany. See also Fig. 16 & 17
21. See page 214
22. Ashton, *The Unknown Shore, a View of Contemporary Art*, p. 205
23. ibid.
24. Schreyach, *Pollock's Modernism*, p. 5
25. Feldman, *Give My Regards to Eighth Street, Collected Writings of Morton Feldman*, p. 4
26. Schreyach, *Pollock's Modernism*, p. 97

Bibliography

'Around Morton Feldman: interview by Robert Ashley, New York City, March 1963', unpublished transcript, Morton Feldman Collection, Paul Sacher Stiftung, Basel.

Ashton, Dore. *The Unknown Shore, a View of Contemporary Art*. Boston: Little, Brown & Company, 1962.

Bois, Yve-Alain, Joosten, Joop, Zander Rudenstine, Angelica, and Janssen, Hans. *Piet Mondrian 1872-1944*. Milan: Leonardo Arte, 1994.

Cage, John. *A Year From Monday*. London, New York: Marion Boyars, 1968.

Cage, John. *I-VI*. Hanover: Wesleyan University Press, 1990.

Cage, John. *The Selected Letters of John Cage*, edited by Laura Kuhn. Middletown: Wesleyan University Press, 2016.

Cage, John, Feldman, Morton. *Radio Happenings I-VI*. Cologne: Edition MusikTexte, 1993.

Cage, John. *Silence*. Cambridge Mass. and London: The M.I.T. Press, 1967.

Cline, David. *The Graph Music of Morton Feldman*. Cambridge: Cambridge University Press, 2016.

Cunningham, Merce. *Changes; Notes on Choreography*, edited by Frances Starr. New York: Something Else Press, 1968.

Cunningham, Merce. *Summerspace* (1958). https://dancecapsules.mercecunningham.org/overview.cfm?capid=46033 accessed 7 July 2021

Feldman, Morton. *Atlantis*. New York, London, Frankfurt: C.F. Peters Corporation EP 6906, 1962.

Feldman, Morton. *Crippled Symmetry*. New York, London, Vienna: Universal Edition UE 17667, 1983.

Feldman, Morton. *Durations 2*. New York, London, Frankfurt: C.F. Peters Corporation EP 6902, 1961.

Feldman Morton. *Essays*, edited by Walter Zimmermann. Kerpen: Beginner Press, 1985.

Feldman, Morton. *For John Cage*. New York, London, Vienna: Universal Edition UE 17623, 1982.

Feldman, Morton. *Four Instruments*. New York, London, Frankfurt: C.F. Peters Corporation EP 6966, 1965.

Feldman, Morton. *Give My Regards to Eighth Street, Collected Writings of Morton Feldman*. Cambridge MA: Exact Change, 2000.

Feldman, Morton. *Intersection 2*. New York, London, Frankfurt: C.F. Peters Corporation EP 67076, 1962/1998.

Feldman, Morton. *Intersection 3*. New York, London, Frankfurt: C.F. Peters Corporation EP 67076, 1962/1998.

Feldman, Morton. *Interview with Howard Skempton* (1977), http://www.cnvill.net/mfskempton-interview.pdf accessed 15 February 2018.

Morton Feldman. *Ixion*. Version for ensemble New York, London, Frankfurt: C.F. Peters Corporation, 1962, EP 6926.

Morton Feldman. *Ixion*. Version for two pianos New York, London, Frankfurt: C.F. Peters Corporation, 1962, EP 6926a.

Feldman, Morton. *Last Pieces*. New York, London, Frankfurt: C.F. Peters Corporation EP 67076, 1963/1998.

Feldman, Morton. *Morton Feldman Says: Selected Interviews and Lectures 1964-1987*, ed. Chris Villars. London: Hyphen Press, 2006).

Feldman, Morton. *Morton Feldman in Middelburg, Lectures and Conversations*, edited by Raoul Mörchen. Cologne: MusikTexte, 2008.

Feldman, Morton. *Projection 1*. New York, London, Frankfurt: C.F. Peters Corporation EP 6945, 1961.

Feldman, Morton. *Projection 5*. New York, London, Frankfurt: C.F. Peters Corporation EP 6962, 1964.

Feldman, Morton. *The Straits of Magellan*. New York, London, Frankfurt: C.F. Peters Corporation EP 6919, 1962.

Feldman, Morton. *Two Pieces for Two Pianos*. New York, London, Frankfurt: C.F. Peters Corporation EP 6916, 1962.

Feldman, Morton interviewed by Han Reiziger, VPRO Radio, 5 November 1985, transcription by John Snijders.

Greenberg, Clement. *The collected Essays and Criticism, Vol. 2, Arrogant Purpose, 1945-1959*, edited by John O'Brian. Chicago, London: University of Chicago Press, 1986.

Greenberg, Clement. *The collected Essays and Criticism, Vol. 3, Affirmations and Refusals, 1950-1956*, edited by John O'Brian. Chicago, London: University of Chicago Press, 1993.

Greenberg, Clement. *The collected Essays and Criticism, Vol. 4, Modernism with a Vengeance, 1957-1969*, edited by John O'Brian. Chicago, London: University of Chicago Press, 1993.

Guston, Philip. *Philip Guston, Collected writings, lectures, and conversations*, edited by Clark Coolidge. Berkeley, Los Angeles, London: University of California Press, 2011.

Higgins, Charlotte. *Greek Myths, a New Retelling*. London: Jonathan Cape, 2021.

Krasner, Lee. *Interview 27 June 1978*. Jackson Pollock and Lee Krasner papers, circa 1905-1984. Archives of American Art, Smithsonian Institution, Washington, https://www.aaa.si.edu/collections/items/detail/interview-lee-krasner-19237 accessed 06 August 2018.

Nattiez, Jean-Jacques. *The Boulez-Cage Correspondence*, translated and edited by Robert Samuels. Cambridge: Cambridge University Press, 1993.

O'Connor, Francis V. *Jackson Pollock*. New York: The Museum of Modern Art, 1967.

O'Hara, Frank. Essay for 'New Directions in Music 2', reprinted in *Vertical Thoughts, Morton Feldman and the Visual Arts*, edited by Seán Kissane. Dublin: Irish Museum of Modern Art, 2010.

Oteri, Frank. *A Chance Encounter with Christian Wolff*, Interview at the Greenwich House Music School, New York, 11 January 2002, https://nmbx.newmusicusa.org/a-chance-encounter-with-christian-wolff/ accessed 15 January 2018.

Patterson, David. *Cage and Beyond*: an Annotated Interview with Christian Wolff, in *Perspectives of New Music*, Vol. 32, No. 2, Summer 1992.

Revill, David. *The Roaring Silence, John Cage: a Life*. New York: Arcade Publishing, 1992.

Rosenberg, Harold. *The Tradition of the New*. New York: Horizon Press, 1960.

Schreyach, Michael. *Pollock's Modernism*. New Haven: Yale University Press, 2017.

Silverman, Kenneth. *Begin Again, A Biography of John Cage*. New York: Alfred A Knopf, 2010.

Snijders, John. "That is not freedom, that is taking license: The pitfalls in performing Morton Feldman's graphic scores" in *The Aesthetics of Imperfection in Music and the Arts*, Edited by Andy Hamilton and Lara Pearson. London: Bloomsbury, 2021.

Suzuki, Daisetz Teitaro in http://sweepingzen.com/d-t-suzuki-bio/ accessed 13 July 2018.

Villars, Chris. *Morton Feldman Works*, http://www.cnvill.net/mfworks.pdf accessed 25 July 2018.

Wolff, Christian. "Taking Chances," *Music and Musicians*, May 1969.

Recordings
Morton Feldman. *Five Pianos,* with Morton Feldman, Harrison Birtwistle, Stephen Savage, Roger Smalley & John Tilbury, recorded 5 January 1973 at St John's Smith Square, London, https://www.cnvill.net/mffivepianos.htm accessed 18 July 2021.

Morton Feldman. *Ixion*, with Eos Ensemble, cond. Jonathan Sheffer, recorded 29 July 1996 at Manhattan Center Studios, NYC, on *Music for Merce*, Catalyst 09026-68751-2.

Morton Feldman. *Ixion*, with John Cage & David Tudor, recorded October 1958 in Stockholm, on *Music for Merce, Vol. 2*, New World Records 80712.

Morton Feldman. *Ixion*, with Kristine Scholtz & Mats Persson, recorded August 2002 in Stockholm, on *Morton Feldman, Complete Works for Two Pianists*, Alice Musik Produktion ALCD024.

Morton Feldman. *Piano Three Hands, Two Pianos, Vertical Thoughts 1*, with Morton Feldman & Ingrid Lindgren, recorded 14 January 1969, Studio 3, Swedish Broadcasting Corporation, Stockholm, https://www.cnvill.net/mflindgren.htm accessed 18 July 2021.

Morton Feldman. *Two Pieces for Three Pianos*, with Morton Feldman, Robert Moran & Loren Rush, recorded 24 January 1969, https://archive.org/details/C_1969_01_24 , accessed 18 July 2021.

Morton Feldman. *Why Patterns?*, with Morton Feldman, Jan Williams & Eberhard Blum, recorded 17 December 1978, State University College, Freedonia, New York, on Morton Feldman: The Viola in my Life, New World Records 80657.

Acknowledgements

I am very grateful to a whole host of people who have made this book possible. Especially Christopher Fox and Katherine Hambridge for reading early versions and giving me indispensable advice, Steven Aalders for all the inspiring conversations we had on painting and Feldman's music and for reading through and commenting on the first and the final draft, and Richard Rijnvos for listening when I had no clear idea what I was doing and getting me back on track.

I want too, to extend a big thank you to all those with whom I have had enlightening, interesting, and stimulating conversations about art and music or who were able to clarify all kinds of things that were out of my reach or beyond my initial comprehension. To name but a few: Tom Benson, Jane Bustin, David Connearn, Laurence Crane, Susanna Eastburn, Andy Hamilton, Tim Hodgkinson, Julian Horton, Patricia Lent (Merce Cunningham Trust), Felix Meyer (Paul Sacher Stiftung), Keith Miller, Martita Slewe, Jobina Tinnemans, and Kees Visser, and last but not least, Gordon Shrigley for inviting me to write *Ixion* and being ever so patient with my record amounts of procrastination along the way.

Finally, of course this book could not have been written without the continuous inspiration I get from Feldman's compositions, lectures and writings and I owe him an enormous amount of gratitude for making my life as a musician so much richer.

Marmalade Publishers of Visual Theory

Series editor: Gordon Shrigley
Drawing Theory

Series designed by Christian Küsters of CHK Design, London
Studio photography by Ferdinand Carabott
Printed and bound in the United Kingdom by Biddles Books
Distributed by Central Books, London
Supported by Durham University

ISBN 978-0-9933373-5-2

First Edition of 250